42 KNEE EXERCISE FOR QUADS
52   "   "   FOR HAMS

CURES
FOR
COMMON
RUNNING
INJURIES

ALSO BY THE AUTHOR

Podiatric Sports Medicine (Futura, 1975)
The Running Foot Doctor (World Publications, 1977)

CURES
FOR
COMMON
RUNNING
INJURIES

BY STEVEN I. SUBOTNICK, D.P.M., M.S.
Illustrations by Stanley G. Newell, D.P.M.

ANDERSON WORLD, INC.

Mountain View, California

Library of Congress Cataloging in Publication Data
Subotnick, Steven I., 1942-
   Cures for common running injuries.

    1. Running—Accidents and injuries. 2. Running
  —Accidents and injuries—Prevention. I. Title.
RC1220.R8S9   617'.1027   78-64383
ISBN 0-89037-155-5

I dedicate this book to my parents,
Ruth and Leonard Subotnick.

Contents

LIST OF ILLUSTRATIONS

Foreword

Runners carry on a strange love-hate affair with pain. On the one hand, they court it, embrace it, brag about how well they deal with it. At the same time, they fear pain, cower in its presence and resent the limits it puts on their running.

A runner might explain this quirk by saying he sees pain two ways. Good pain is the normal, temporary result of effort; it is a pleasant ache that follows hard work well done. Bad pain is the kind that lasts long enough to interfere with running; only when it slows or stops him does a runner admit to being injured.

Runners always have been, and maybe always will be, injured in rather large numbers. Surveys by *Runner's World* note that two in three of them get hurt each year. This happens because running is what it is and runners are what they are. The sport attracts limit-pushers and urges them to find their breaking points, where good pains turn bad.

Despite the progress made in sports medicine the last few years, runners keep getting hurt in the same old ways and numbers. The difference now is when they break. New techniques of prevention and treatment simply allow runners to find their limits at 50 miles a week instead of 30, or seven minutes a mile instead of nine. When cures are found here, they'll crack at 70 miles and six minutes.

The apparently self-destructive nature of runners confounds most doctors. The runners come to them only in desperation, after prayer, home remedies and witchcraft have failed. The injury is too far advanced by then to be treated quickly, but the runner still expects a miracle. If he doesn't find it soon enough, he finds another doctor who'll tell him what he wants to hear. That is, anything but those two awful words, "Stop running." At the first sign of healing, the runner tests himself like an impatient farmer who pulls up his crop to see if it's growing.

This tends to strain a doctor-patient relationship. The doctor suspects the patient of sabotaging his treatment plan, while the runner thinks all doctors want to steal his favorite activity.

Fortunately, there are signs now that both sides can make peace. One reason is that more and more doctors are running, and therefore understand a runner's mixed feelings about pain. Another reason: the podiatrists.

The foot specialists have stepped in to cool hostilities between runners and doctors. They have brought techniques that work–treatment centered on the feet, which absorb most of the blows of running, and treatment aimed at causes instead of symptoms.

As important as the right techniques, however, is the podiatrists' right attitude. That is, a doctor's first duty is to keep runners running, not to tell them, "If it hurts to run, don't do it." Podiatrists offer hope at a time when too many other doctors advise runners to surrender.

I'd heard plenty of "don't run" advice before I was introduced to podiatry. One physician told me when I had a chronic heel injury, "Take a week off." When I returned and told him I hadn't improved, he said, "Well, then, lay off for a month." That's when I went to podiatrist Steve Subotnick.

"That's nonsense," Dr. Subotnick said. "You could rest for a year, and nothing would change. As soon as you started to run again, your heel would hurt. You have a mechanical problem that can only be corrected by mechanical means."

He corrected me. That was six years ago. I can't say I've run happily ever after, because I still have the self-destructive tendencies common to runners. But I can say I probably added six more years to my running life by putting my feet in Steve Subotnick's hands.

The benefits flowed two ways. Subotnick helped a thousand other runners get back on their feet, and they helped him in return. They taught him the fine points of sports podiatry, and they taught him that if he was to understand them, he too had to be a runner who hurt himself the same ways.

I have watched Steve Subotnick mature as a runner and running doctor since I limped into his office and came away whole again. His book represents all he has done and learned in the six years when he hasn't only cared *for* runners, but has cared *about* them, too.

Joe Henderson

PART I

WHY RUNNERS GET HURT

1

Your Injuries, My Injuries

As I sit here on the floor, trying to talk myself into stretching, and I reflect on the six years since I ran my first fun-run with Bob Anderson and Joe Henderson in Los Altos, California, many thoughts pass through my mind. This is the second run I have had today. My first was eight miles at noon. This one was four miles in the evening--very slow, very relaxed, and it gave me a chance to think. I came home from the run feeling at peace with myself and able to think about this book, about runners, the running movement and injuries. Why do runners get injured? Why is there as high as an 80 percent dropout rate in the first two weeks among beginners? Why do twenty-five million people run in the United States, and why in the world are there a million long-distance racers?

I think about myself, about my right knee which is, for the first time in eight months, without pain. I think about the little adjustment of the orthotic device in my shoe which appears to have made all the difference, and I wonder—is it that simple, or was the knee just ready to heal on its own?

I think about the past eight months of running with pain—of days with pain while sitting, when rising, and when trying to walk. I think about the past six years with at least one major injury a year and, more commonly, two a year--injuries which made running difficult, caused me to seek medical attention and to investigate the reasons for my injuries.

3

I am a podiatrist, a running podiatrist. I have been running for the past six years. I have been involved almost from the start in the sports medicine movement for runners. I remember when sports medicine and sports podiatry were in their infancy, and I remember when we knew very little about running injuries. I remember when runners would get injured and go to a doctor who gave them a simple order—"Don't run." I remember patients coming to my office, telling me that I must find a way to keep them running. Running was the most important thing they did during the day, and they begged me to find an answer.

We now have answers. Each year, I know more and more about running injuries that afflict my patients. Each year, I become more knowledgeable and perhaps wiser. That is the reason for this book. Here, I tell why I may think differently than I did in my first book for World Publications (*The Running Foot Doctor*) and, in fact, differently from my textbook (*Podiatric Sports Medicine*).

This book talks about injuries of overuse, injuries of abuse, injuries of too-much-too-soon, injuries of absent-mindedness (the day-dreaming runner who steps off a curb and sprains his ankle), injuries of the enraged runner who chases a dog and finally kicks it and strains a muscle in the back of his leg, injuries of the young and injuries of the old, injuries of the uninitiated and injuries of the pro.

But before I can talk of injuries specifically, I must talk about the mechanisms of injuries, the biomechanics of injuries and those more subtle causes—the body that just won't take any more stress, the accumulated microtrauma.

2

The Mechanics of Motion

Biomechanics is the study of the mechanics of motion, the biology of motion. It allows someone like myself, a sports medicine podiatrist, to listen to complaints of athletes, then to examine the athletes and put pieces together to decide if there is a reason why the injury occurred other than simple abuse of the body.

Is there pain in the right heel because there is a short right leg, and the runner is taking a longer stride with the right leg to catch up with the longer left leg?

Is there pain in the right kneecap when the athlete is running on the left side of the road, and does this pain go away when the direction is reversed? In other words, does the camber of the road change the footplant, causing the foot, leg, and knee to work differently?

Is there pain when running counterclockwise on a track, and does it go away when running clockwise?

These are examples of how I might use the history or chief complaint, and correlate it with biomechanical findings. What you need to know, then, if you are to understand your injuries are some of the basics of biomechanics as well as the basic structure of the lower extremity. This gives you a relatively good idea of how you function.

7

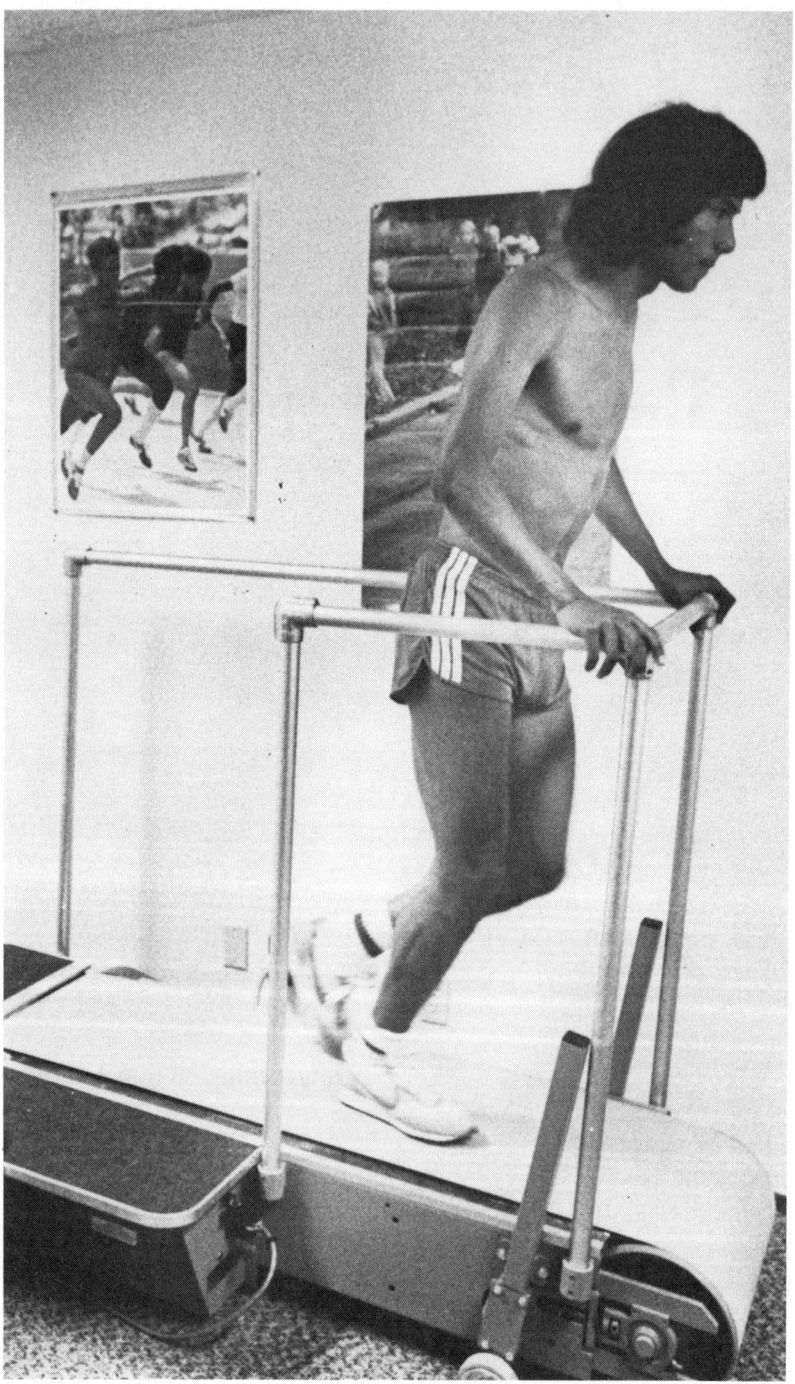

It is important for you first to realize how the body transforms various rotations into meaningful and purposeful forward progression. You should think of your leg and lower extremity as an adjustable strut. This allows bending motions to occur at the major joints, which result in forward motion. This adjustable strut also allows the center of gravity to stay relatively level during running.

The foot acts as a universal joint to let the forces on the lower extremity be absorbed at the level of the foot. When you are walking and running, the swing leg moving through the air is internally rotating (*fig. 1*). This means that the foot and kneecap rotate from a position where they are facing outward to facing inward. If we picture the right leg swinging through space, then the right big toe would move toward the midline of the body with internal rotation of the right leg. This internal rotation remains as the heel hits the ground and for 10 to 20 percent of the total time the foot is on the ground.

However, the internal rotation cannot continue with the foot against the ground, because of the cohesive and abrasive forces between the ground and the foot and shoe. In other words, it is impossible for you to rotate your foot internally against the ground without tearing the sole off your shoe. The foot and shoe are relatively fixed on the ground.

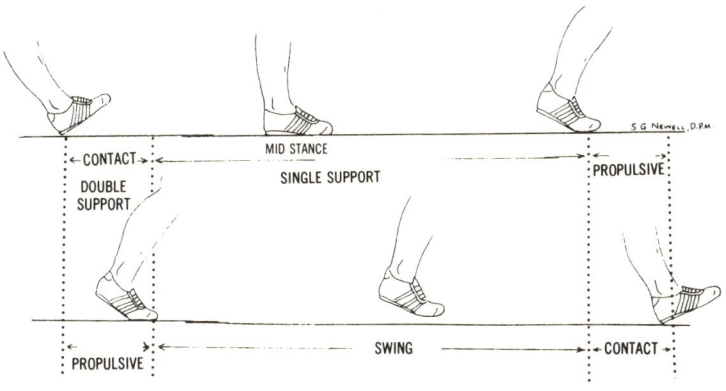

Figure 1
Coordinated Gait Cycles of Both Lower Extremities (Walking)

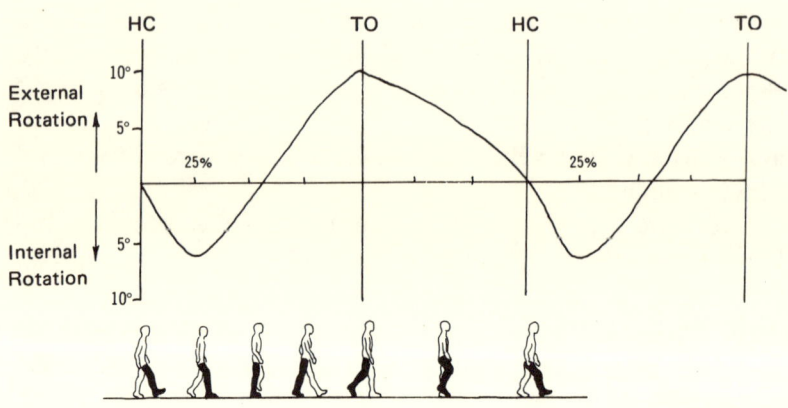

Figure 2
Rotations of the Legs and Effects Upon the Foot

It is important, then, for some mechanism in the foot to allow the rotation to be absorbed in the foot. In the joint just below the ankle, the subtalar joint, internal rotation occurs as the foot flattens or pronates. Thereby, the foot absorbs or transforms the internal rotation of the leg into the pronation of the foot (*fig. 2*).

Pronation at the subtalar joint is synonymous with a lowering of the arch and a more flexible foot. This, of course, is useful because it allows the foot to act as a mobile adapter so that the foot and body above it can adapt to varying surfaces. You can see how important this is for running on irregular surfaces such as golf courses or mountain trails.

This, however, can be a problem when running on smooth, hard, man-made surfaces such as concrete or asphalt. The reason for this is that you contact on the outside of the heel with the heel actually tilted outward from 4 to 8 degrees (*fig. 3*). The heel then tilts the other way as the foot pronates. The foot has a tendency to overpronate, and all of the pronating motion available may be used (*fig. 4*). Thus, when the foot over-pronates, it is almost impossible for it to become a rigid lever at toeoff. The foot never becomes the strong lever it must be as the body weight passes over the ball of the foot.

What I have said is bound to confuse you, as it would have

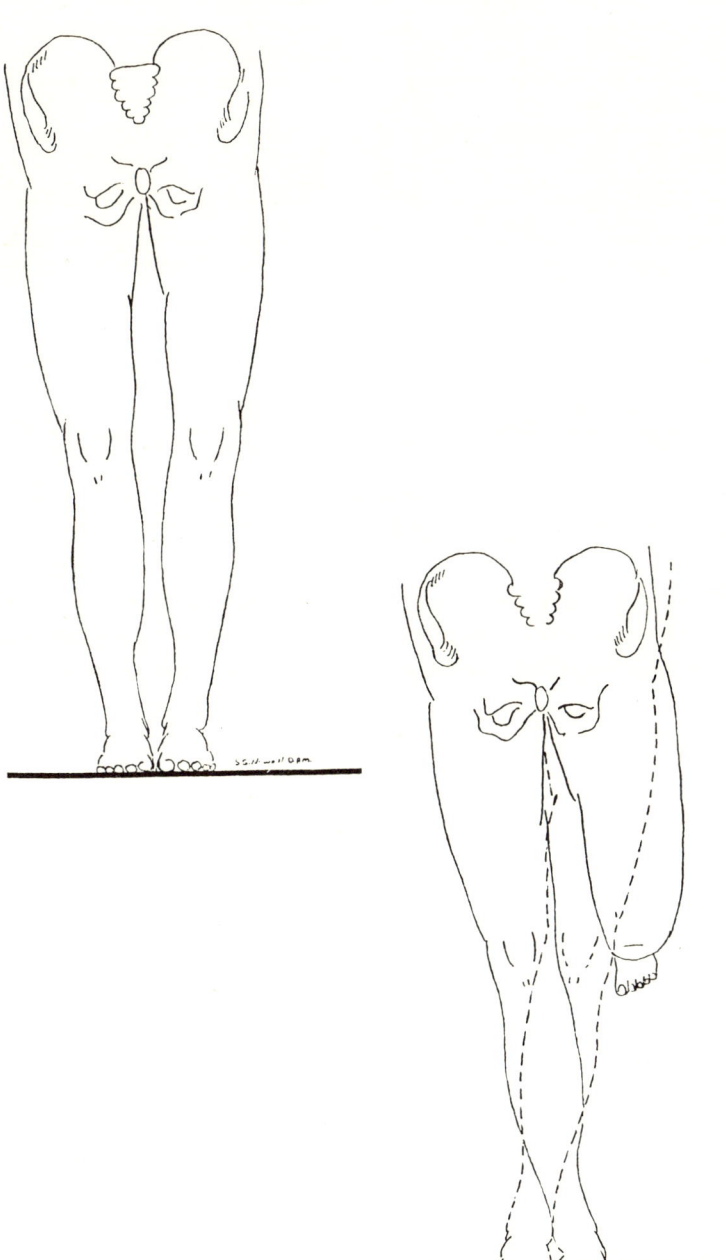

Figure 3
Crossover Variation in the Angle of Gait During Running

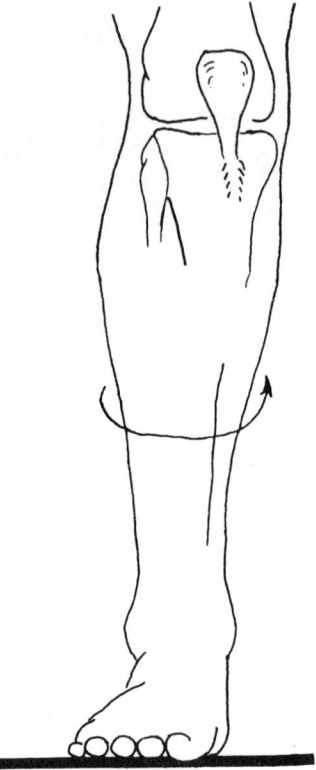

Figure 4
Prolonged Pronation of the Foot

confused me several years ago. So let me go over it again in simpler terms:

The foot is supposed to act as a mobile adapter from that brief moment when the heel first touches the ground until the whole foot touches the ground. The leg internally rotates when it is swinging through space and for a brief time when the foot first touches the ground. The leg then externally rotates. At the same joint where pronation takes place, supination then occurs. With supination, the foot changes from a mobile adapter to become a neutral structure at midstance and then a rigid lever at toeoff.

Neutral means that if you cut all the muscles, tendons, and ligaments going through the foot and put weight on both feet, the arches would not collapse. In other words, the joints and bones line up in a manner that there is structural integrity within the arch arrangement of the foot (*fig. 5*). It's pretty hard to reproduce this neutral situation in everyday activities, but it is a theoretically perfect position which must be appreciated to understand functional foot control.

At toeoff, the weight of the body is over the ball of the foot, and there must be flexibility at the ball where the toes join it. You do not really require a forceful toeoff, using your muscles and tendons to drive the toes through the supporting surface, because your body weight throws your body forward off the metatarsophalangeal joint (*fig. 6*).

There are basic differences between walking and running. One is that in walking full body weight goes through the foot

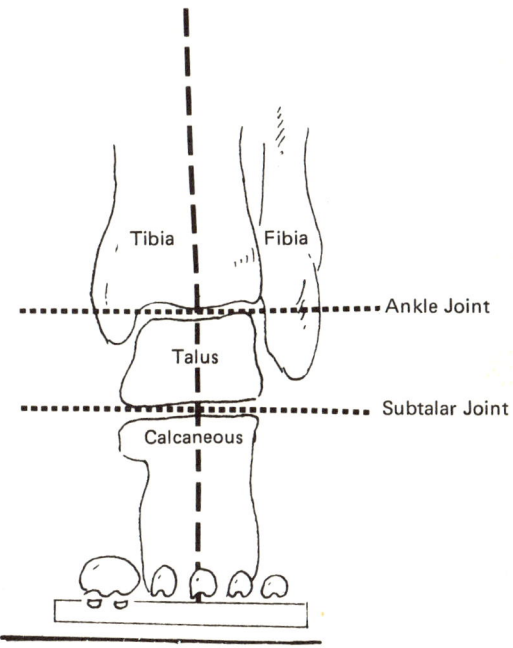

Figure 5
The Normal Foot and Leg

Figure 6

The Gait Cycle in Running

(*fig. 3*). This means if you weigh 150 pounds, about 150 pounds go through one foot and then the other as you walk. When both feet are on the ground, 75 pounds go through each foot.

But during running, either one foot is on the ground or you are flying through space. Because you are flying, you land with much more force going through your foot—about three times your body weight, or 450 pounds if you're a 150-pounder. When running downhill, this increases to almost four times the body weight. Running is definitely much more stressful than walking.

Now, I ask you to perform a simple test. Stand up, put most of your weight on your right foot, and collapse your right arch as much as you can. When you collapse your right arch, you notice that your right leg, kneecap, thigh, and hip internally rotate. When your hip internally rotates, you notice that the front of it bends downward, and the back of it rises on the right side. When you do the opposite maneuver, externally rotating your leg, you notice your arch becomes higher, and your knee and hip point out. Likewise, the front of your hip on the right side rises, and the back of your hip lowers.

What you have done with internal rotation of the leg and lowering of the arch is pronate your lower extremity. What you have done with external rotation of the leg and raising of the arch is supinate your lower extremity. It is easy to understand, then, that the arch of the foot, the subtalar joint, and the joint even closer to the toes, the midtarsal joint, are pronatory-supinatory joints that work about very complex triplane axes. Any foot deformity or any problem in footplant can cause problems anywhere along the lower extremity due to the abnormal rotations which are basically controlled by the foot.

The most frequent problems I see are in runners who have low-arched feet which pronate at contact and never recover to become neutral or high-arched feet at toeoff (*fig. 4*). This is an unstable lever system, and causes abnormal rotations and fatigue of the muscles which have to work overtime to support the arch—all in vain because of the tremendous stress going through the lower extremity.

The opposite of this is equally important—the high-arched foot which does not absorb shock, does not act as a mobile adapter, and thus causes shock waves to travel farther up the leg, leading to problems in the knee, thigh, or back.

The sequence of pronation and then supination dissipates much of the contact stress. Pronation is necessary, as it allows shock waves to be delivered into space and not into the lower extremity. Supination is important, because it allows the foot to be a rigid lever with the integrity of the arch being supported by the foot more than by the body.

A further concept must be understood. This again is difficult to explain. When you are running, the foot should land directly beneath the center of gravity. If you are running on a track where you can see your footprints, each foot should land on a line drawn down the center of the track (*fig. 7*). This stops the body from wobbling side to side. It also allows the body to be balanced above the foot rather than supported. When you have abnormal running form, you may do more supporting than balancing, and this leads to fatigue. Fatigue leads to injury.

Stride variation may further complicate the problem. Your foot should land directly beneath the center of gravity when you are running. In other words, your foot swings forward, then begins swinging backward and lands under your center of gravity as your body catches up with your foot. When this happens, the ground neither forces your body back nor propels your body forward, but the body gently rolls over the foot. If you overstride, the ground pushes you back and you wear out the rear of the shoe more than if you are running properly. If you understride, you have a tendency to run on the ball of your foot.

But it is not all that simple. The faster the pace, the more weight is put on the ball of the foot and the more time is spent in the air (*fig. 8*). Also, people with high-arched feet or dropped forefeet may be more comfortable running on the balls of their feet. The important thing is for their feet to land under their centers of gravity and for them not to understride or overstride. Those people with more normal feet or lower-arched feet should run heel-foot-toe. Some people will be more comfortable landing more flatfooted, or gently on the outside of their feet, and then rolling toward the inner border of their feet. The key is that the foot lands at zero acceleration under the center of

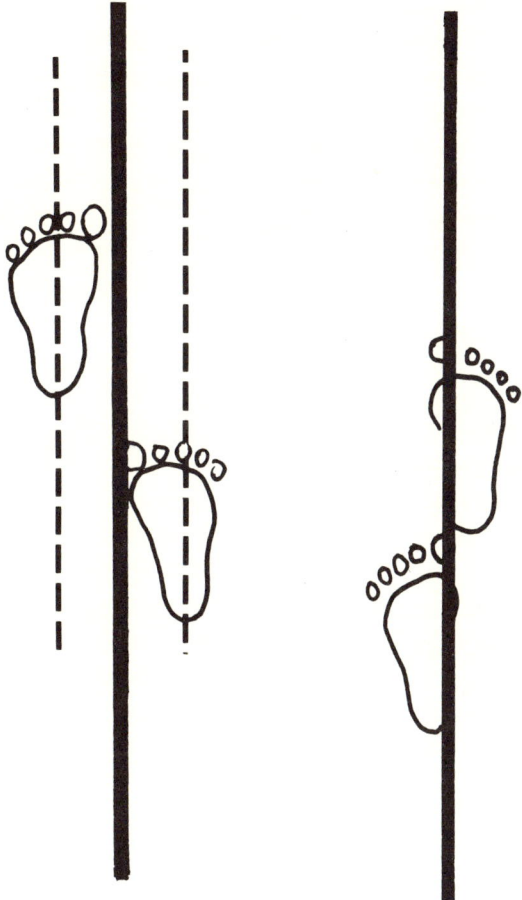

Figure 7
Walking Vs. Running Footstrike

gravity. If you try to change this and your structure is not ready for it, you may end up with an injury.

You may wonder why you always wear out the outside of the shoe heel. Everybody is supposed to wear out the back part of the heel. In fact, you should have maximum stress going through your heel about a quarter-inch outside of the center on the back of the heel.

Since your feet land directly under the center of gravity in running and are far apart in walking, there is more wear on the

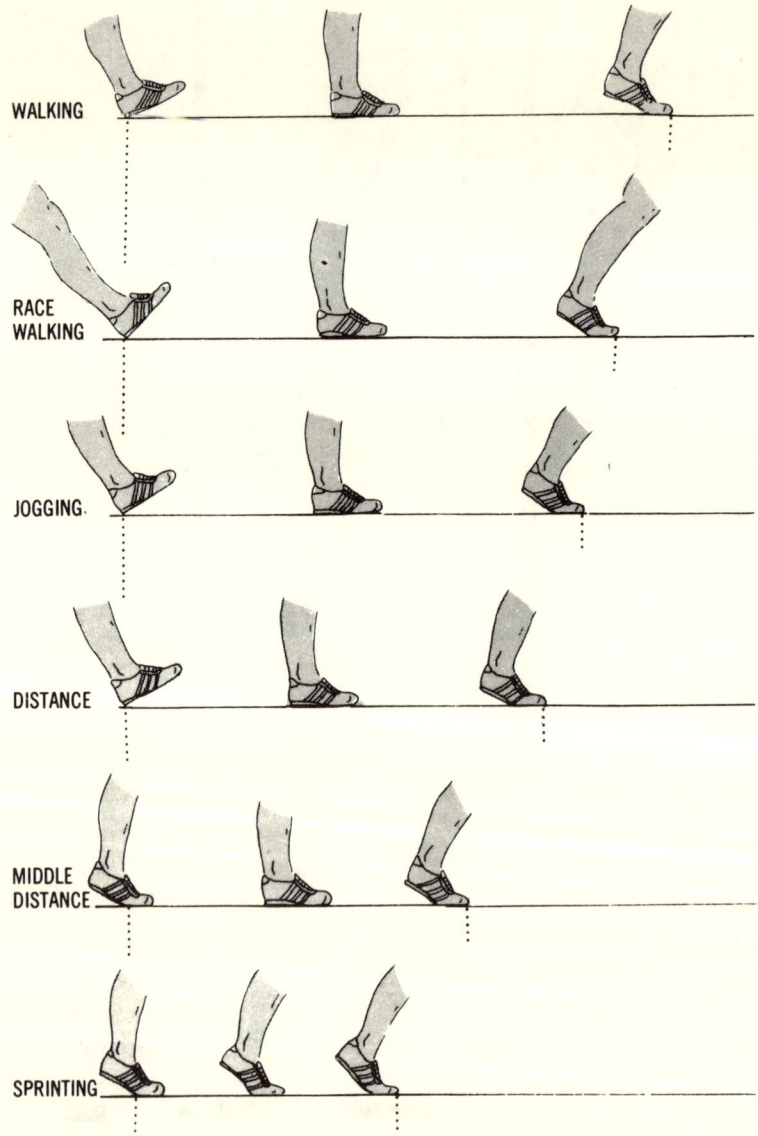

WALKING

RACE WALKING

JOGGING

DISTANCE

MIDDLE DISTANCE

SPRINTING

Figure 8

Comparison of Walking and Running Gaits

outside of the runner's shoe heel. You become more bowlegged when you run, which is natural and normal. This "functional varus" or increase in your normal bowleggedness causes more pronation to take place. Even people with normal lower extremity structures may end up with overuse injuries due to overpronation, because the act of running itself has a built-in hazard. This is not to say that running is dangerous or that running is not beneficial. There simply are stresses in running you must understand if you are to run injury-free.

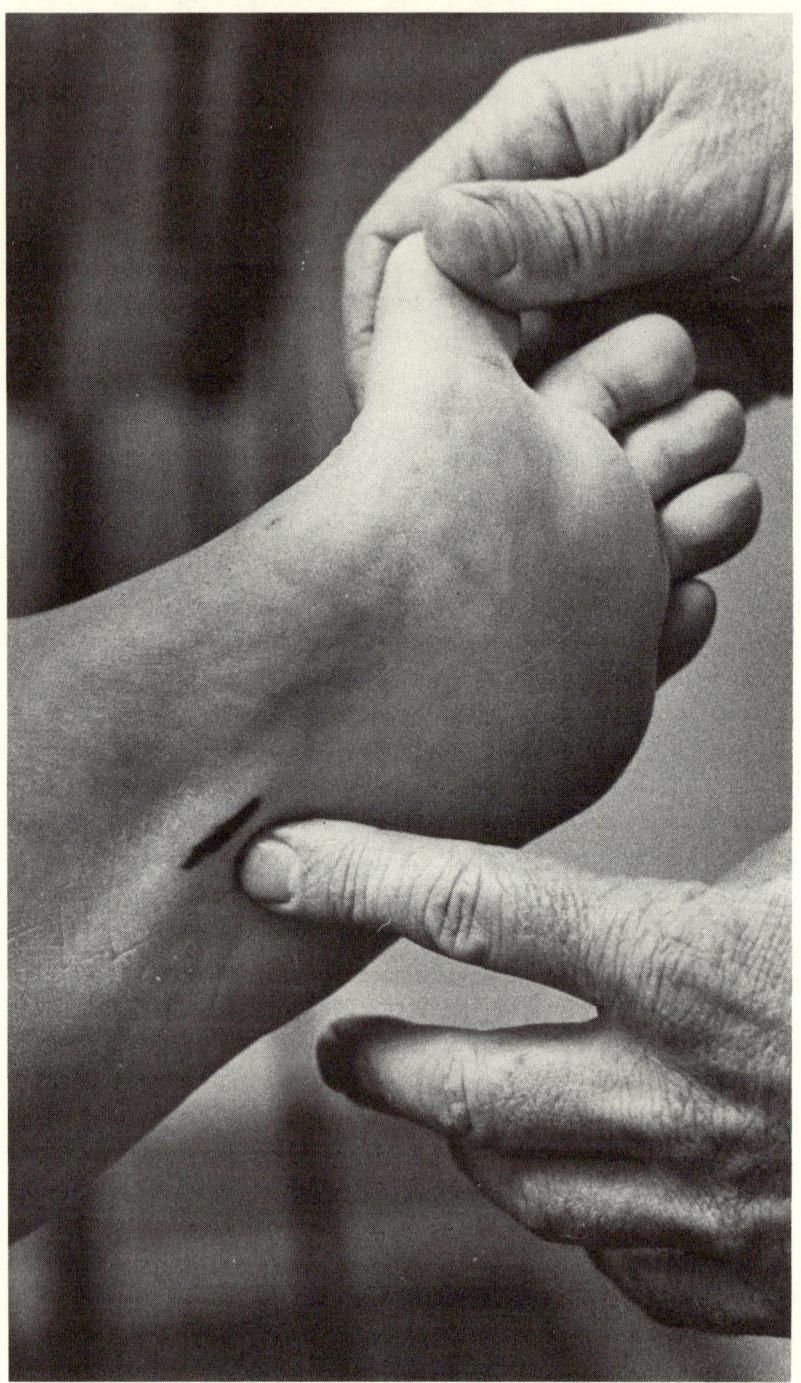

3

Mechanical Defects

Various foot and leg types can be described in terms of the joints of the lower extremity and the angles that its components make with each other.

An example of this is the term varus, which indicates that a part of the body faces toward the midline. Thus, a tibial varum (*fig. 9*) means that the tibia bone of the leg has such angulation that it swings the foot toward the midline of the body. Tibial varum implies bowleggedness; when the inside ankle bones are together, the knees are apart. The opposite of this is tibial valgum, which means that when the legs are together the ankle bones are apart. With valgum, the structure involved faces away from the midline of the body (*fig. 10*).

To carry this a step further, let me describe the forefoot. A forefoot varus means that the bottom of the foot is angulated so that it faces the midline of the body (*fig. 11*). Forefoot valgus is the opposite, the bottom of the foot facing away from the midline. Thus, a forefoot varus allows for a gap between the inside of the foot or inner arch and the ground when the foot is neutral. A forefoot valgus lets the opposite occur.

The joint beneath the ankle joint is the subtalar. A subtalar joint varus places more weight on the outside of the heel bone, because the heel faces toward the midline of the body. A subtalar joint valgum causes the heel bone to face the opposite way.

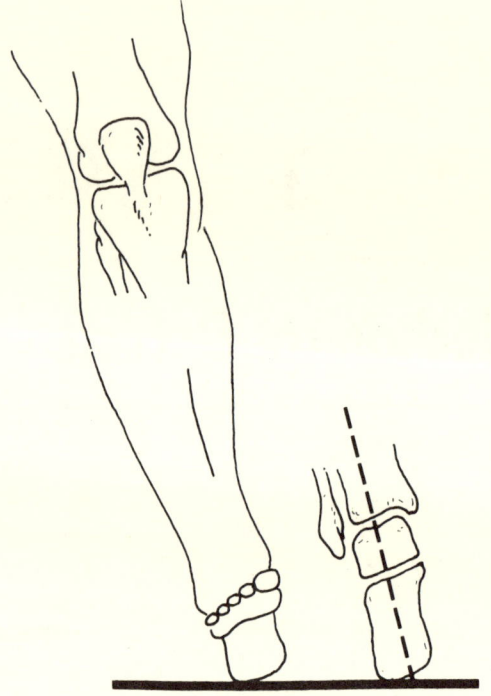

Figure 9
Tibial Varum

If this isn't complicated enough, we also have to think in terms of what the angular deviations are from the norm. The norm has the leg bones perpendicular to the ground. Likewise, the heel bone (calcaneus) is perpendicular to the ground and parallel to the lower one-third of the leg. When all the weight is placed through the outside of the foot, all the metatarsal heads rest on the ground, and the midtarsal joint (where the forefoot and rearfoot meet) is locked and neutral. This allows the bony architecture of the foot to support the body weight when you are standing on both feet and both are neutral. When this happens, there is a normal medial-longitudinal arch. Also, there is alignment of the knee joint with a straight-line pull over the femur (thigh bone), and the quadriceps (strong muscles of the thigh) work properly.

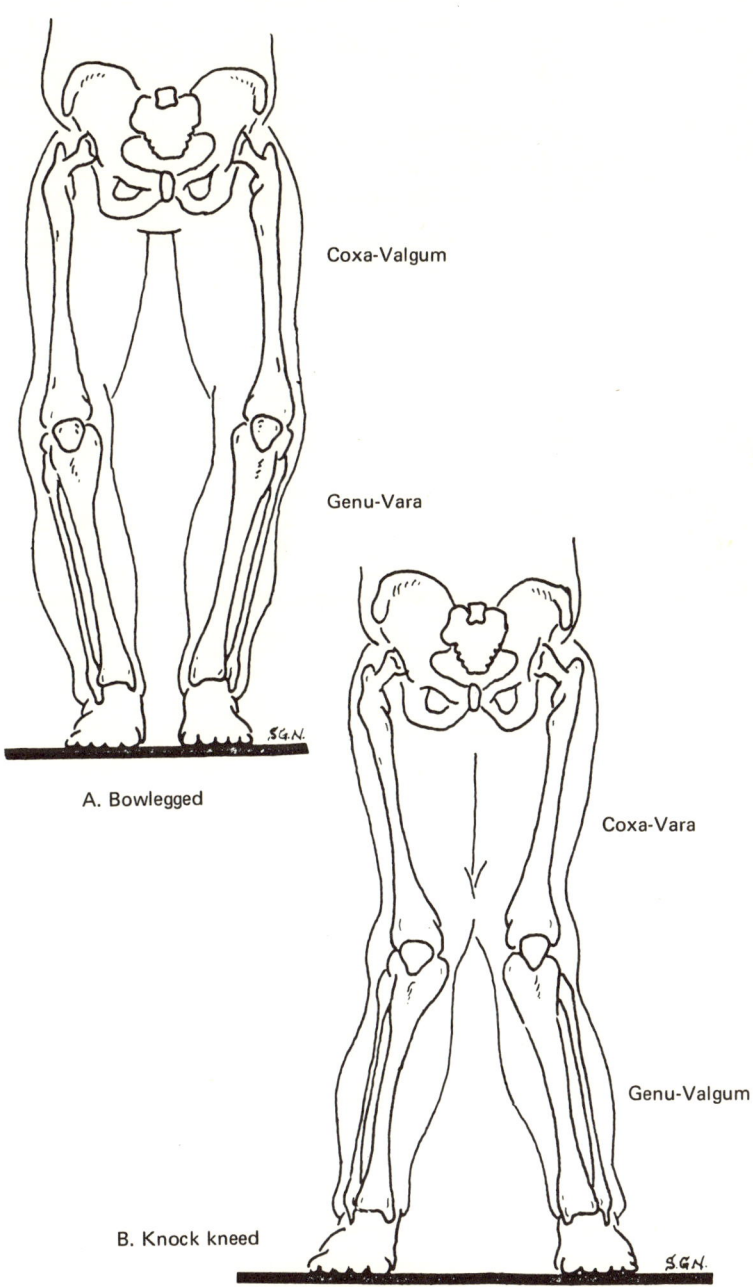

Coxa-Valgum

Genu-Vara

A. Bowlegged

Coxa-Vara

Genu-Valgum

B. Knock kneed

Figure 10
Frontal Plane Deformaties

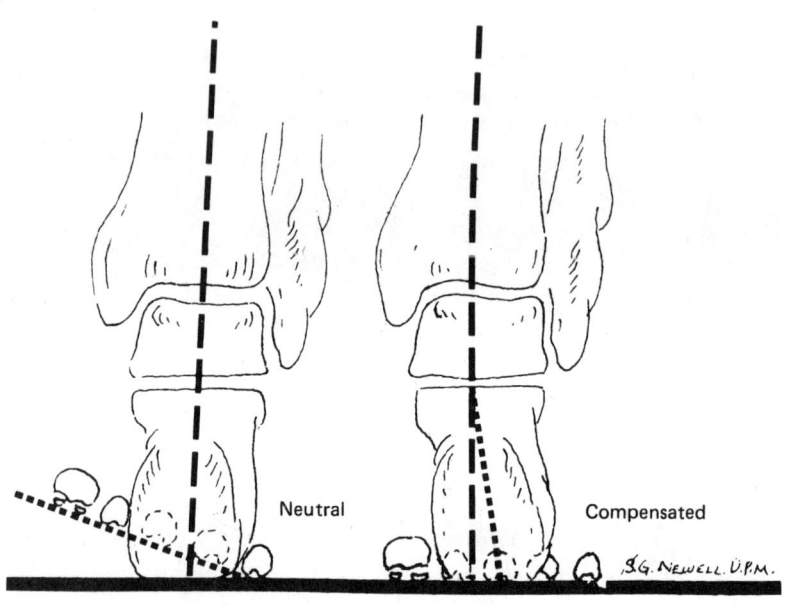

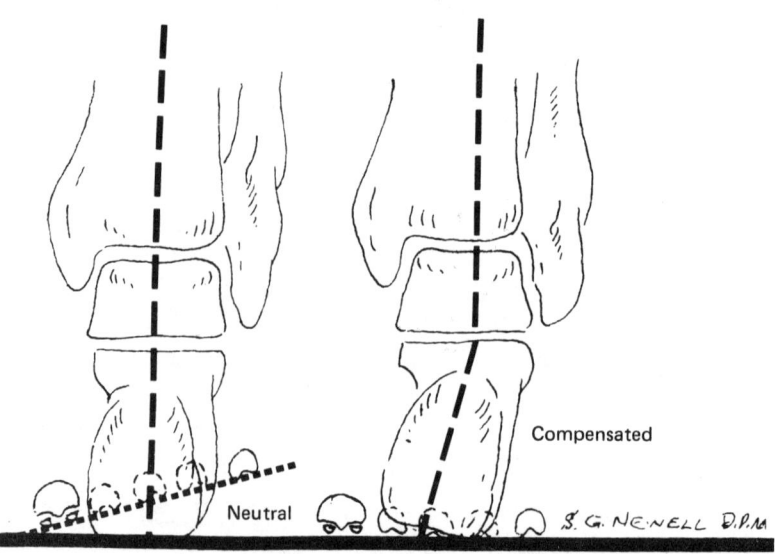

Figure 11

*Forefoot Varus and Compensation (Top); Forefoot Valgus and
Compensation (Bottom*

Most people have a bit of bowlegged deformity or tibial varum when walking; the average for our population is 4 to 5 degrees. In running, varum increases by 3 to 4 degrees, because the foot contacts toward the midline of the body rather than along parallel lines as in walking. Along with the three-to-four degree·functional varus of running and the tibial varum of 4 to 5 degrees, there may be a little bit of varus in the subtalar joint.

When the subtalar joint is neutral, you can press up as hard as possible along the outside border of the foot, and the midtarsal joint will be maximally pronated and locked. When this happens, all the metatarsal heads rest on the ground, and the arch will not collapse. The more the subtalar joint is inverted (supinated), the higher the arch is and the less motion is available from the midtarsal joint. Thus, the foot becomes very rigid and does not absorb shock well, but works well to allow for a good toeoff. The more the subtalar joint is everted (pronated), the lower the arch, the more mobile the foot and the more motion available in the midtarsal joint. If more motion is needed in the midtarsal joint, the subtalar joint must pronate first (*fig. 12*).

Along with subtalar varum, there may be deformities of the midtarsal joint. There may be what I have described as forefoot varus, more commonly referred to as Morton's foot. The opposite deformity is forefoot valgus.

A forefoot-varus foot has excessive mobility along the first and inner metatarsals, and must pronate to allow the metatarsals to reach the ground. When this pronation takes place, the subtalar joint unlocks, the foot becomes unstable, then the leg must internally rotate.

A forefoot valgus is the high-arched, rigid foot which does not absorb shock well. This foot is likely to have a callus or pain beneath the first metatarsal head.

Foot types are further complicated by talking about the arch itself. Many people have high-arched feet with dropped forefeet. These runners tend to run on the balls of their feet or to be toe runners and tend to form calluses under their metatarsal heads. They may also have a tight plantarfascia, that structure between the heel bone and the metatarsal heads on the bottom of the foot which may be strained.

The opposite of this is a low-arched foot which is excessively

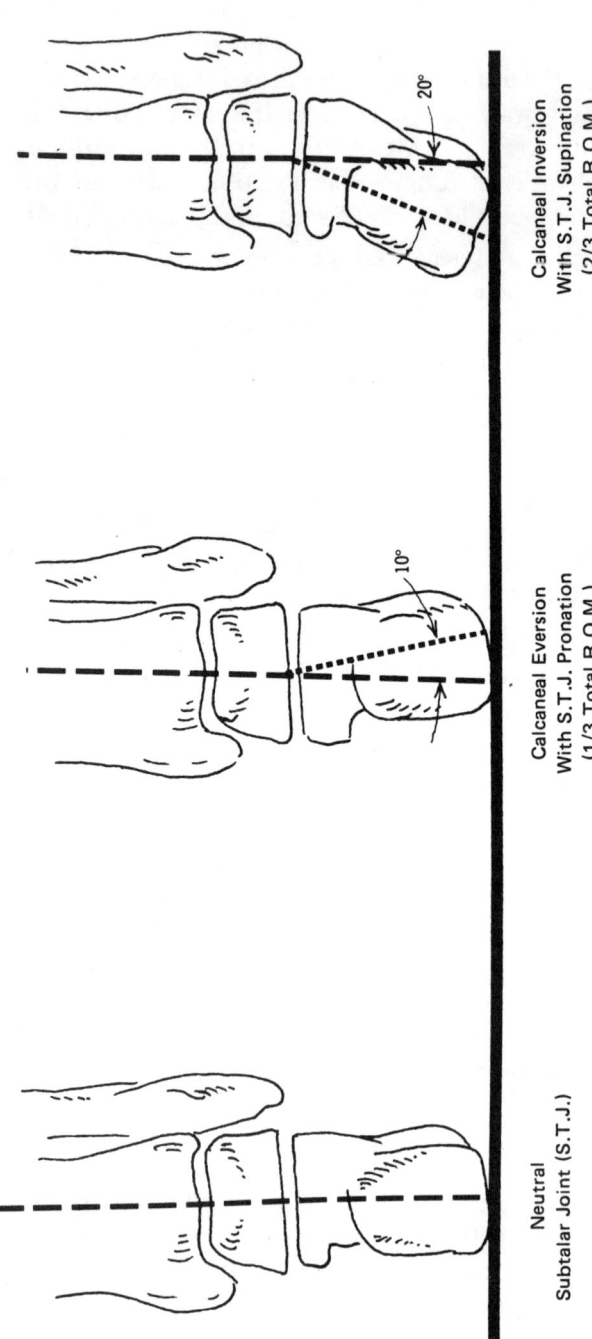

Neutral
Subtalar Joint (S.T.J.)

Calcaneal Eversion
With S.T.J. Pronation
(1/3 Total R.O.M.)

10°

Calcaneal Inversion
With S.T.J. Supination
(2/3 Total R.O.M.)

20°

Figure 12

Neutral Position of Subtalar Joint and Range of Motion

mobile. This foot often has a long second toe and short first toe, meaning that the first metatarsal can't bear weight properly and the foot must pronate to allow the metatarsals to reach the ground.

Some people have angulations between the toes and the metatarsal bones that make it difficult for them to walk straight ahead and, in fact, cause them to toe in or toe out when they walk. Some are born with metatarsals which toe in, causing them to run on the outsides of their feet and to have pain when wearing shoes that are built on a conventional last. The pain often is over the fifth metatarsal head or the styloid process of the fifth metatarsal, the outer border of the foot. They may also have pain over the inside aspects of the greater toes because the shoes try to deform these joints.

Further problems occur because of the rotational problems in the leg or hip. A runner may be born with or may develop tightness of the soft tissue around the hips, causing the feet to toe in. He may have toeing-in on one side and toeing-out on the other, which makes running rather difficult and causes abnormal function and overuse injuries.

As we get older, we tend to lose our range of motion at the hips, and many older runners tend to toe out. Toeing-out gives more stability when you are walking but makes you unstable when you are running by reducing the weight-bearing ability of the knee.

Along with soft-tissue problems, one may have actual bony problems which cause abnormal rotations. All of these abnormalities are magnified in running.

4

Three Times the Trouble

A "rule of three" applies to running. Since three times more force goes through your foot when you run than when you walk, everything wrong is multiplied by three. Thus, if you have, as most long-distance runners do, only mild imbalances in your foot—say, two degrees of forefoot varus, two degrees of subtalar joint varus and four degrees of tibial varum—this would not ordinarily cause problems. But when we multiply all of this by three to account for the tripled force going through the foot when you run, you have enough biomechanical abnormality to cause a true overuse injury such as runner's knee, Achilles tendinitis, or arch strain.

We also see that runners who have nothing wrong while going 10 miles per week may have problems at 20 miles per week. In other words, there appears to be more than a straight-line increase in the stress going through the body of a long-distance runners. Most runners with fairly good structure and fairly good running shoes can do fairly well at 10 to 20 miles per week, but when they increase their mileage from 20 to 30 miles weekly they may start getting overuse injuries.

Therefore, runners with as little as three-to-four degrees of deformity may require some type of biomechanical device or functional foot orthotic. This orthotic is made from a cast of the foot and holds the foot in a neutral position at midstance. It encourages the foot to assume its own neutral position for

stability to occur. Orthotics are not a crutch but a biomechanical device which helps the body function properly around a stable fulcrum.

I see runners who have been doing a pain-free 40 miles a week, increase their mileage to 60 or 80 then start having overuse injuries. While they may benefit from orthotics, their overuse injuries quite often are secondary to too much running, too soon or cumulative stress that their bodies just cannot tolerate.

On the other hand, many people have enough biomechanical deformities to cause some aches and pains during everyday activities. These people definitely need orthotics even before they begin a running program. For instance, somebody with hypermobile flat feet or six to seven degrees of forefoot varus needs orthotics even if he is only going to run only a mile a day.

The point here is that runners break down for many different reasons—some inherent to the stresses of the activity, some caused by inherent weaknesses of the individual, most the result of these two factors combined.

PART II

HOW RUNNERS GET HURT
... AND GET WELL

5

Knee Injuries

Robert McGrath, a 44-year-old runner and tennis player, complained of pain at the front aspects of both knees. He also had some pain in the back of each thigh after running. He noted that the outside back portions of both shoes had excessive wear. At the time, he was running 15 miles a week on the roads, including some hills.

McGrath's medical history was unremarkable, and there was no reason to suspect that he had a generalized arthritic problem. (X-rays confirmed that he had none.)

I examined him at length and noticed that the muscles going into his kneecaps, the quadriceps, were somewhat weak. Further examination showed no pain over the joint lines, and there was no sign of damage to the cartilage inside the knees with standard orthopedic testing. The ligaments of the knees were strong.

My evaluation showed there was no locking, catching, or giving out of the knees, and that he could do squats without any problems. There was just slight pain underneath the kneecaps. His feet pronated, due to his Morton's foot configuration, his kneecaps were somewhat unstable, and the kneecaps went to the outsides of his legs. I told him this was a patellar compression syndrome or mild lateral displacement of the kneecaps. The stronger the medial quadriceps muscles were, the less tendency he would have to do this.

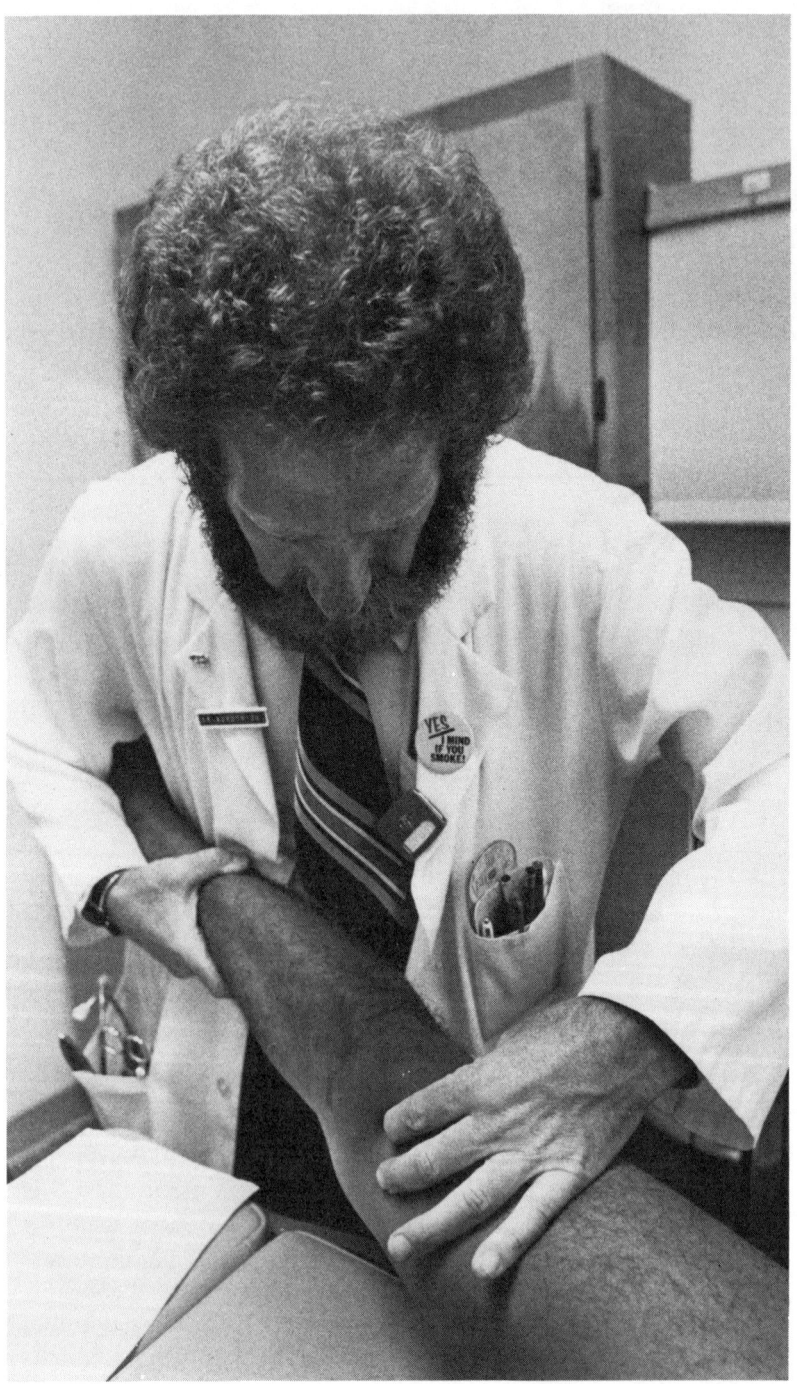

I advised him to do quadriceps exercises, contracting these muscles with the legs straight to a count of twenty or until a burning sensation began, repeating this exercise twenty times in the morning and twenty in the evening. I further suggested that he avoid running downhill. I dispensed soft temporary orthotics to stabilize the foot and, thus, the knee.

Robert returned five months later, noting that his running had been extremely comfortable for most of that time. But in the past two weeks, the knee pain had come back. He noticed that his soft foot supports were beginning to wear down and didn't offer as much control as they originally had. He figured it was about time to get permanent orthotics, since he had given his soft supports a good try.

I examined him and noted that the strength of his quadriceps had deteriorated somewhat with the return of his runner's knee problem. I again told him to do quadriceps exercises, and to use elastic tape underneath his kneecaps to lift them and prevent strain on the undersurface where the cartilage was rubbing abnormally. The soft supports were built up again, and he was casted for permanent orthotics to be used for running and everyday activity. He received a firm pair of orthotics for his everyday shoes and a more flexible pair for running.

I was pleased that McGrath was able to correlate the return of knee pain with the wearing down of the temporary supports. This led me to believe that as long as he was getting proper foot support, which prevented abnormal kneecap displacement, he would be asymptomatic. This also helped substantiate my general belief that many of the runners' knee problems are helped with proper foot placement and strong quadriceps muscles.

Robert McGrath's case demonstrates that soft supports do work well, and should be used until both the patient and the doctor firmly believe more permanent orthotics would be beneficial.

KNEECAP PAIN

The knee is a complicated joint, and the kneecap or patella is part of this mechanism. The kneecap is a sesamoid bone, there to increase the mechanical advantage of the knee joint.

Having this bone on top of the joint makes the extensor action of the knee more efficient. In fact, it converts the knee in this area into a first-class lever.

The outside surface of the patella is covered by skin and fat, and there are sacs called bursae under the skin. The large prepatellar bursa at times becomes inflamed and causes a great deal of pain, although the injury is quite minor and treatment is relatively simple. There are other bursae around the knee joint and the kneecap itself.

The undersurface of the kneecap has two joint surfaces called facets which meet the femur, the thigh bone. The patella must track straight up and down in order for the cartilage on the kneecap to move smoothly over the cartilage of the femur. When the kneecap does not ride smoothly over the femur or when it rides to the outside, this causes abnormal wear of the cartilage and the familiar pain under the kneecap generally called runner's knee. Over-use injuries about the patella can be classified more precisely according to where the pain is and the mechanism behind the injury. I'll say more about this later.

The first symptom of kneecap problems is usually a gradual onset of pain. At first, there may not be pain; it is more a tightness. This then becomes dull aching and finally turns into pain.

The pain often is mileage-related. It appears that repetitive and accumulated stress causes the pain under the kneecap. Some people can run 20 miles a week and never have knee pain, but when they go up to 30 miles a week they begin to hurt. This means there is too much stress at 30 miles for the structure to handle, and this causes abnormal pressure on the patella or patellar cartilage.

There may eventually be some softening of the cartilage. If there is enough abnormal tracking of the kneecap and the runner continues to run with pain, this softening may cause some cracking or fissuring of the cartilage. This is true chondromalacia. When cartilage damage is present, there is a grinding sensation under the kneecap. Any pressure on the knee which pushes the kneecap to the outside or inside causes excruciating pain.

Once the aching becomes pain, there usually is more pain going up or downstairs, or on hills. Level surfaces are easier to walk upon. The runner notes that when the leg is straight there is relatively little pain, but as soon as he bends beyond 15 degrees the pain becomes almost unbearable. Many athletes relate that they can ride a bike but cannot run with their knee problems. Hill riding, however, causes pain.

Some athletes connect the onset of their patellar pain with running on hills, especially downhill. The reason is there is *four times* the body weight going through the leg on downhill runs compared to three times body weight on level runs. Also, the runner tends to overstride going downhill, causing more shock to shoot up the leg and to the area of the kneecap. If he has an unstable foot with excessive pronation, this causes increased instability of the kneecap and increased abnormal cartilage wear.

Now that you know the warning signs of runner's knee, you should know more about the patella itself. At the superior pole or upper aspect of the kneecap, the extensor mechanism which straightens the leg inserts into the patella. Thus, when you extend your knee, you use the quadriceps muscles. The extensor mechanism is extremely important, since it stabilizes the kneecap.

The most important muscle of the quadriceps group is the vastus medialis which stops the kneecap from rolling to the outside of the leg. When the kneecap does slip to the outside, this is called lateral subluxation or lateral displacement (*fig. 13*). This motion of the kneecap is largely responsible for the runner's knee syndrome. A strong vastus medialis muscle helps prevent this from happening.

A straight or extended knee is a stable knee. (Race walkers, who must straighten and lock their knee with each stride, seldom have kneecap problems.) The more the knee is bent, the more unstable it becomes and the greater the likelihood of runner's knee developing. Many orthopedic specialists feel the knee should never be bent more than 90 degrees when the body is carrying an excessive load. I agree with this.

At the inner aspect of the kneecap, the vastus medialis, ligaments and tendons form what is called the medial retinaculum. At the outside of the knee is the lateral retinaculum. These are tough, fibrous bands which help the extensor mechanism stabilize the kneecap. At the inferior pole or bottom of the kneecap is the patellar tendon. This tendon inserts into a

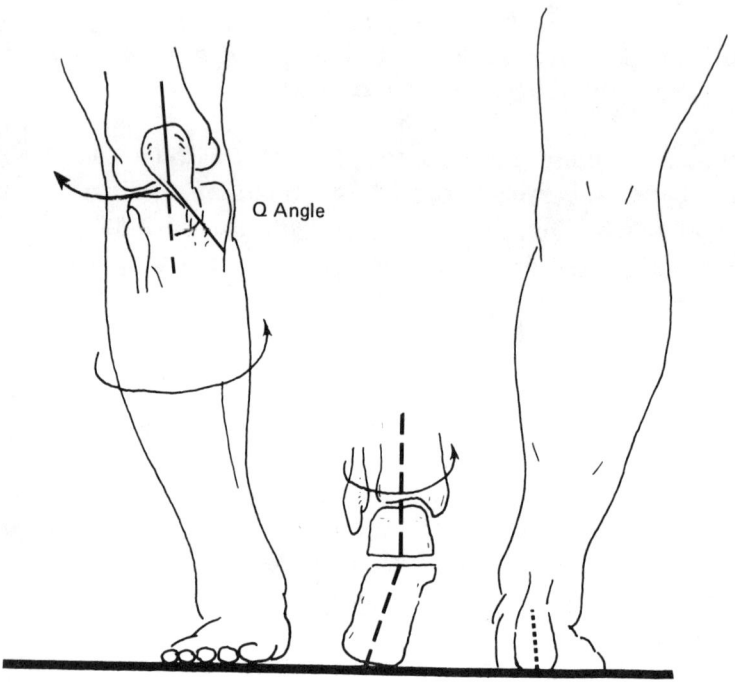

Figure 13
Patellar Subluxations with Pronation of the Foot

tubercle on the tibia bone. The patellar tendon may be injured as part of the overuse injury called jumper's knee.

What are the classifications of patellar problems in runners? The most common is patellar compression syndrome. As far as I can tell, this name was given by Dr. Stan James, an orthopedist from Eugene, Oregon. At least he was the one who explained this to me. Patellar compression syndrome is when there is pain and aching underneath the kneecap, but there is not a lot of crepitation, that sandpaper sensation or sound that occurs when the kneecap moves over the femur. Likewise, there is little softening or fissuring of the cartilage on the undersurface of the patella. The pain can be just as bad as when cartilage pathology is present, but there is little actual damage. This overuse problem usually responds to some form of orthotic foot control and exercises to build up the quadriceps mechanism, especially the vastus medialis. At times, elastic taping over the patellar tendon to lift up the kneecap is helpful. As a last resort, surgical lateral retinacular release may help.

Less common, but far more serious, is true chondromalacia of the patella. This is where there is actual pathology on the undersurface of the kneecap; the cartilage is fissured or fractured and softened. Chondromalacia often is present in runners who have unstable knees not only when they are running but also when they walk. Once it occurs, it takes quite some time to recover. Recovery usually requires extensive exercises as well as orthotic foot control and, indeed, abstinence from running until pain is absent during walking and jogging. If there is deformity in the leg or kneecap itself, activities other than running might have to be substituted. Race walking, swimming, and cross-country skiing are excellent alternatives. At times, surgical procedures by an orthopedist are necessary for advanced, nonresponsive chondromalacia.

Lateral subluxation is a third classification of patellar problems. This means the kneecap moves to the outside of the leg as the leg rolls in during foot pronation. However, excessive lateral subluxation is usually rare in runners. A mild or moderate runner's knee problem is often a combination of patellar compression syndrome and mild lateral subluxation. It responds readily to reduced training and running at slower speeds. Orthotic foot control and proper exercises for the extensor mechanism are mandatory. Downhill running should be avoided.

True lateral subluxation of the patella means that the kneecap itself is deformed, and the undersurface of the patella does not have its normal facet shape. The kneecap may actually jump to the outside of the femur bone and may have to be put back in place. This difficult problem is best treated by an orthopedic surgeon.

Jumper's knee is the fourth classification of patellar injuries. It is usually over the patellar tendon at the inferior pole of the kneecap. There is pain because the tendon has pulled on the bone, causing a small rupture of this area. X-rays are often utilized since they show a small spur on the inferior surface of the patella. At times, there may be a form of jumper's knee at the superior pole of the patella where the quadriceps mechanism inserts. This may result from running faster than normal, running hills, jumping or kicking. Treatment consists of rest, taping, and orthotic foot control. Rehabilitative strength exercises are helpful.

Quadriceps exercises should be done by every athlete who has even a hint of a patellar knee problem. I tell my patients to lie or sit down and place a rolled towel behind the knee joint. This causes the knee to be flexed about 15 degrees. I then have them put one leg on top of the other and straighten out the bottom leg, using the upper leg as a weight (*fig. 14*). They hold this contraction to a count of twenty. They feel the vastus medialis to make sure that it is contracted and hard, especially near its attachment on the kneecap. After doing twenty of these quad sets, I have my athletes flex their knee to stretch out the quadriceps mechanism (*fig. 14*). This is done simply by pulling the foot until the heel touches the buttocks. They then lean forward and pull the foot back, stretching the quadriceps area. If a runner's knee problem occurs during a run, he should stop and do a few quad sets and then stretch the extensor mechanism.

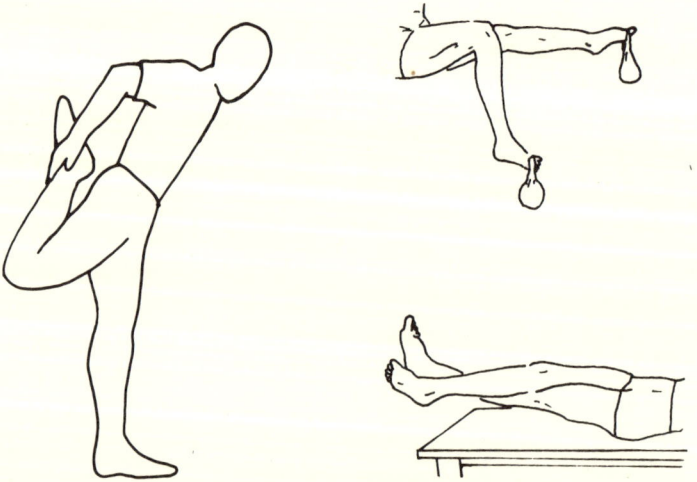

Figure 14
Quad Strengthening and Stretching Exercises

If more strength is necessary after doing quad sets, then I have runners go to a weight program. They start with five-pound weights for the quad sets and build up to forty-pound weights to build up the extensor mechanism. When they use weights, I tell them to start with the knee flexed from 15 to 20 degrees by sitting on a low bench and having their heel rest on the ground. They have the weight on the ankle and then straighten the leg, holding this position to a count of fifteen or twenty. The most good is done when there is a burning sensation in the quadriceps.

Why and how do orthotics work with runner's knee? Essentially, the runner has an imbalance in the foot, excessive pronation takes place, and the leg must internally rotate. As this happens, the kneecap becomes unstable because the thigh bone has a tendency not to want to internally rotate. A large angle forms between the inferior pole of the patella and the attachment of the patellar tendon; this is called the "Q" angle (*fig. 15*). If it is more than 20 to 25 degrees, whenever the quadriceps mechanism contracts it pulls the kneecap to the outside instead of pulling it straight up and down. This improper tracking causes much of the runner's knee problem. Simply using an orthotic foot device, you stop excessive pronation of the foot and also excessive internal rotation of the leg as the "Q" angle is lessened. There is now a straight pull of the patella.

The long-leg-short-leg syndrome (*fig. 16*) also can cause runner's knee, because the athlete tends to rotate the short leg externally for increased stability. This causes the kneecap to be less stable and more vulnerable to injury. A heel lift balances the leg lengths.

If you have a runner's knee problem, I suggest you stay off hills, run slower, and do quadriceps exercises. You might try using elastic tape underneath the kneecap to lift it up. An elastic knee-sleeve also can be used; fold it in half so that it rests just at the inferior pole of the patella and over the patellar tendon. This causes the kneecap to ride or glide upon a different surface of the femur where no damage takes place and the kneecap becomes more stable. This is much the same as the treatment for tennis elbow.

Two aspirin taken a half-hour before running is an excellent

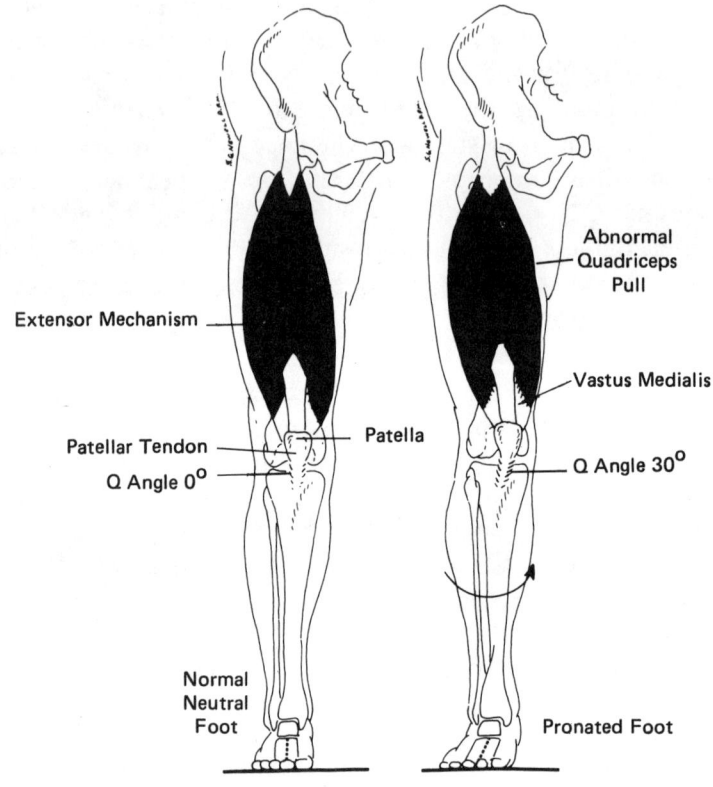

Figure 15
Chondromalacia of the Knee

way to reduce inflammation. Icing the knee for six minutes after running is another good idea. You may have to run every other day instead of daily. Decreasing your speed decreases the amount of flexion and causes the knee to be more stable when you run. (Remember that a straight leg is a more stable one and is less easily injured.)

Orthotic foot control is very helpful. You might try a cheap, over-the-counter support first. If you notice some help with this, then go to a podiatrist and get a more permanent orthotic made. Likewise, you may have just enough imbalance so that it will be stabilized with one of the newer running shoes with a varus wedge and built-in foot support. If you notice some improvement but still have symptoms, see a podiatrist for a custom-made foot orthotic.

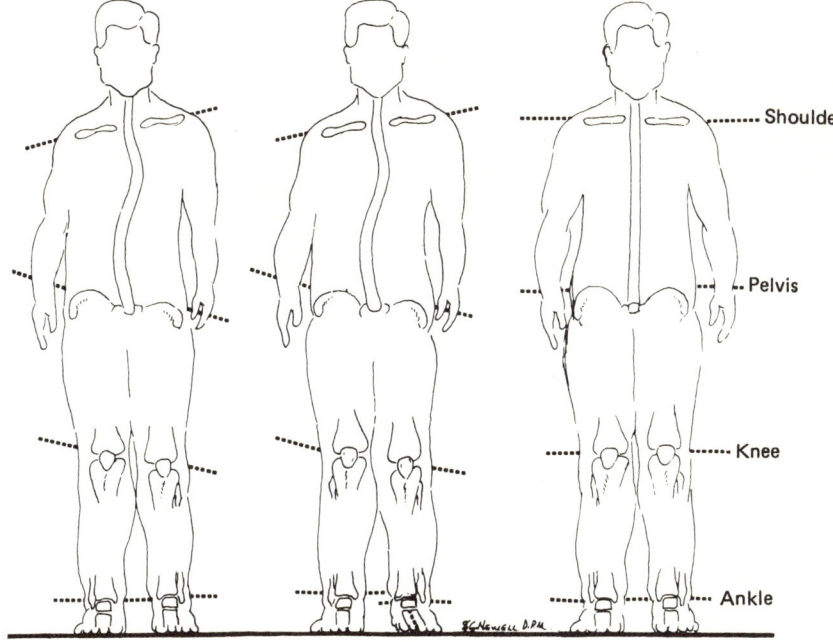

Figure 16
Anatomical Short-Leg (Left), Functional Short Leg (Center),
Disappearance of Functional Short Leg with Orthotic Control (Right)

OUTSIDE OF KNEE PAIN

One of the conditions discussed in the previous section was patellar compression syndrome. This is a tightness of the structure which attaches to the kneecap on the outside of the knee, called the lateral retinaculum. The tightness may also be associated with pain on the outside of the knee near the kneecap which is usually a runner's knee problem.

However, pain on the outside of the knee away from the kneecap may be due to another specific problem. The most common cause of pain here is the iliotibial band syndrome (*fig. 17*). What appears to be happening is a snapping of a tight band of tissue over the bones on the outside of the knee joint. A muscle called the tensor fascia lata begins at the hip joint. It plays an important role in the runner's leg since it stabilizes the outside of the thigh. This muscle soon becomes a thin band

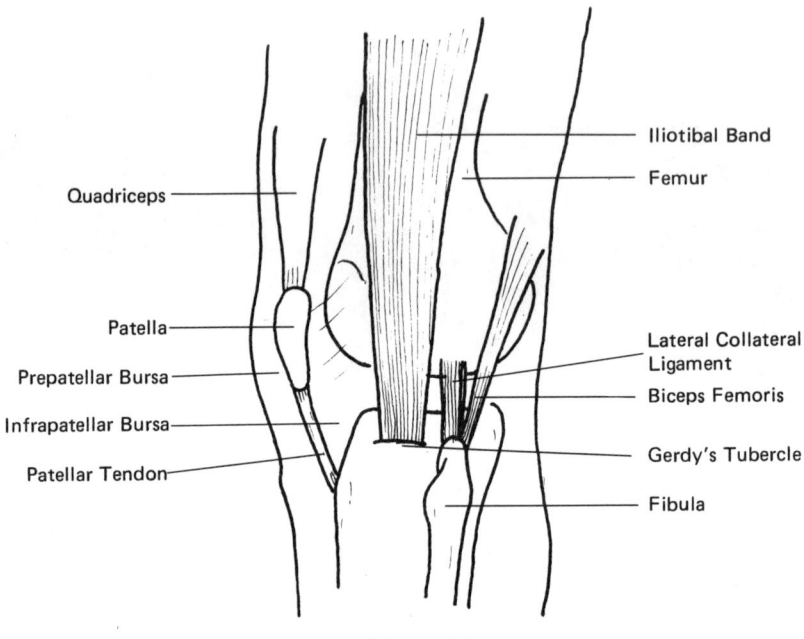

Figure 17

Lateral View of Iliotibial Band "Subluxing" Left Knee

which crosses the knee joint and attaches to the outside of the tibia.

When the knee bends, the band has a tendency to snap forward. This movement of the band may cause a snapping or irritation of the tissue, causing very sharp pain. At times, the pain is so severe it feels as though the knee is going to collapse. This should not, however, be confused with pain on the outside of the knee which is deeper and in the joint itself, and may be due to a damaged cartilage.

It is rather uncommon for running itself to cause damage to the cartilage. Running may cause a flareup of a pre-existing problem such as a torn cartilage from a football injury which then surfaces at the beginning of a running program. But the iliotibial band syndrome is not as serious as a cartilage problem, although the pain may be as severe.

If you look at the outside of your knee while sitting down, then tighten your knee so the muscles in the front of your thigh are as tight as can be, you may see your iliotibial band. While you're sitting, simply move your knee from full extension into flexion and palpate. If you feel a tight band that appears to be snapping and you have pain on the outside of the knee, you have the iliotibial band syndrome.

Iliotibial band syndrome often appears in runners who drastically increase their mileage. The iliotibial band has to work harder than usual and is not used to the increased stress. It gets fatigued and then tightens, and a tightened tendon snaps over the bone. Treatment is to reduce the mileage, stay off hills, and stay away from races until the pain goes away. You can usually run up to the point of pain, then that is it for the day. You have very little choice with this injury, as the pain is severe enough to stop you from running even though the actual damage taking place is minimal.

I had this problem myself (see chapter 11) and found that it was so severe after a marathon I could barely walk up and downstairs; I could not run at all. After resting for two weeks, I could only run one mile a day. It took me a good two months to recover from this injury. The treatment I used was two aspirin a half-hour before running and ice massage for six minutes after running. I also wrapped an elastic bandage around the knee to place compression over it and help minimize the movement of this tight piece of tissue. What really helped, however, were a lot of lateral stretching exercises (*fig. 18*) and a cortisone injection.

If there is foot imbalance or limb-length discrepancy, orthotic foot control is useful. For chronic, resistant causes where there has been inflammatory scar tissue laid down, a mixed cortisone injection along the band may be helpful. However, this injection should not be given into the knee joint. If the doctor is trying to make a differential diagnosis between the iliotibial band syndrome and a problem deep inside the knee joint itself, he can cinch the diagnosis by injecting with local anesthetic and cortisone along the band. If the pain goes away, then it is assumed there is no problem deep within the joint along the cartilage. If the pain is still there, a further orthopedic workup may be needed.

Pain on the outside of the knee can be secondary to a strain of the lateral collateral ligament. This ligament goes from the head

Lateral Wall Stretch   Windmill Stretch

Figure 18
Knee Exercises

of the fibula to the femur farther toward the back of the knee than the iliotibial band. The lateral collateral ligament can be tested by crossing the injured leg over the uninjured leg and then palpating with the fingertips the area that hurts. If the pain arises from the head of the fibula, then you may have a strained lateral collateral ligament. This normally will not be a problem unless you are running on very irregular surfaces or routes with lots of curves. For instance, racing downhill on a curvy cross-country course can strain this ligament. It is also a very common football injury. If you were injured in football, then healed and returned to running, you may aggravate the old injury.

General treatment for pain on the outside of the leg is to cut back on mileage, slow down, and stay off hills. Use aspirin, taking two a half-hour before running, and then use an elastic wrap during the run. Apply ice for six minutes after the run. Do a lot of stretching exercises. If you still do not get better, consider getting new shoes. If this does not help, see a podiatrist and have him examine you to see if there is enough imbalance to warrant an orthotic. At times, anti-inflammatory medication other than aspirin will be necessary. In some cases, an injection with Xylocaine and cortisone will be helpful. Resistant cases may need special orthopedic diagnostic procedures and treatments. Another hint with outside knee pain is to look at your shoes. If you are wearing the outside of the injured leg's shoe more than the opposite shoe, you may be having the iliotibial band syndrome simply by placing more stress on the outside of the knee.

If you have orthotics which were recently dispensed and you notice you are getting the iliotibial band syndrome, you may very well have tight structures on the outside of the knee from too much control. In other words, the orthotics are tilting your foot and leg too much to the outside and actually aggravating the iliotibial band syndrome. If this is the case, have your podiatrist reduce the amount of control in the orthotics.

INSIDE OF KNEE PAIN

Pain on the outside of the knee is often caused by too much tilting to the outside of the leg. Conversely, pain on the inside of the leg or knee is often caused by too much tilting toward the inside, or too much pronation. With pronation of the foot or lowering of the medial longitudinal arch, there is internal rotation of the leg. This can cause strain of the structures on the inner aspect of the knee.

The most common strain on the inside of the knee in runners is bursitis of the pes ansrinus, a structure encompassing three tendons on the inside of the knee. These tendons can rub on each other, or the underlying soft tissue or bone, and cause bursitis—a deep blister. When this happens, the runner feels as though the whole knee may collapse. However, the only real problem is inflammation.

The diagnosis of pain on the inside of the knee can be difficult, because a damaged medial cartilage of the knee can act as pes bursitis. In fact, a pes bursitis can cause swelling which is difficult to differentiate from swelling deep down in the knee joint.

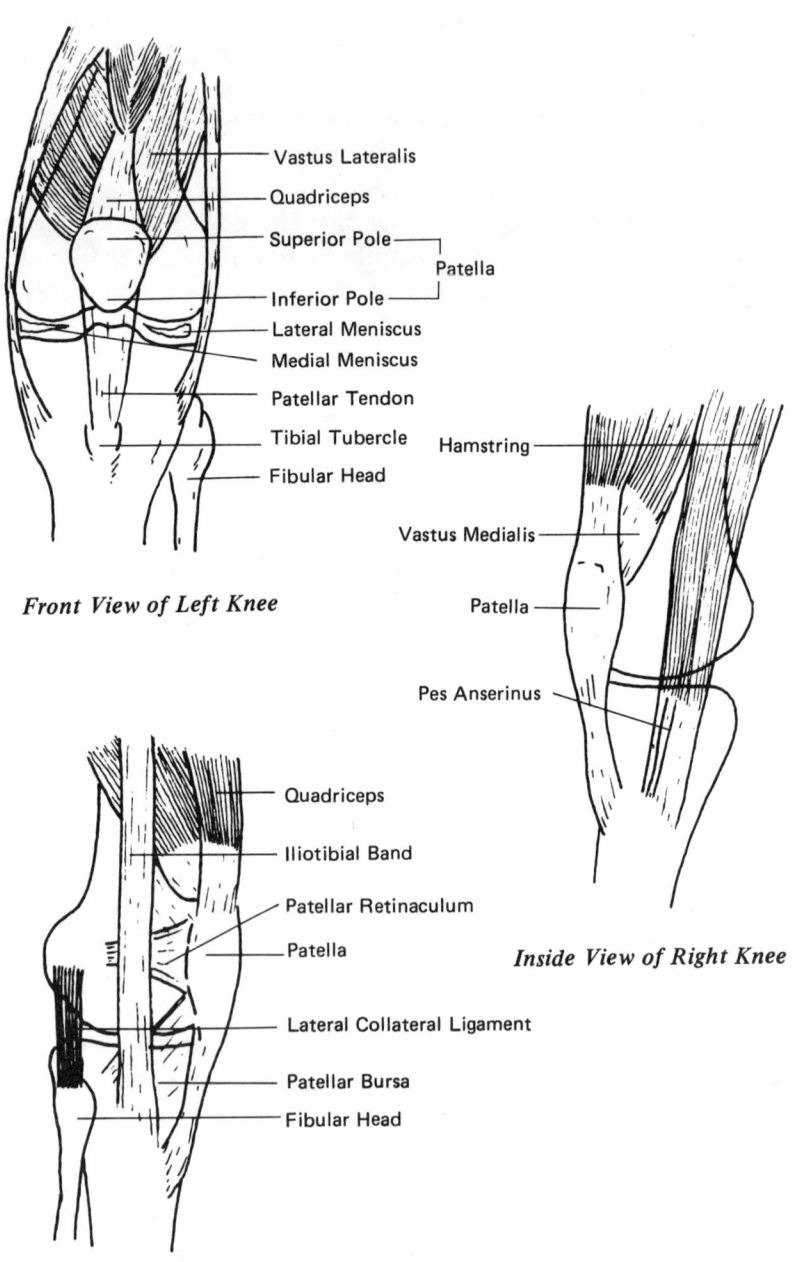

Front View of Left Knee

- Vastus Lateralis
- Quadriceps
- Superior Pole — Patella
- Inferior Pole — Patella
- Lateral Meniscus
- Medial Meniscus
- Patellar Tendon
- Tibial Tubercle
- Fibular Head

- Hamstring
- Vastus Medialis
- Patella
- Pes Anserinus

Inside View of Right Knee

- Quadriceps
- Iliotibial Band
- Patellar Retinaculum
- Patella
- Lateral Collateral Ligament
- Patellar Bursa
- Fibular Head

Lateral (Outer) View of Right Knee

Anatomy of the Knee

The same basic rule applies to the inside of the knee as the outside: Running itself seldom causes damage to the cartilage, but previous injuries may flare up again in the act of running. An example is a football player who sustained injured meniscus of his knee from being clipped. He gave up football, did nothing for the next three years, then took up long-distance running. Lo and behold, the inner aspect of the knee joint starts hurting. This likely is a flareup of the medial cartilage, and the athlete should see an orthopedist for this problem. However, it also may be bursitis of the pes or a capsolitis (joint sprain).

Pes bursitis usually responds dramatically to orthotic foot control. Along with this, anti-inflammatory medications, aspirin, and ice are helpful. Mileage should be reduced. attempts should be made to strengthen and stretch the muscles and tendons of the inner aspect of the knee. A tight elastic band to compress the sore area around the knee is helpful during running. Injections may be necessary to establish the diagnosis and degree of inflammation. If a small amount of local anesthetic will numb the area that hurts and it is outside the joint, there probably is no damage to the cartilage.

You can tell if you have pes bursitis by pressing on the inside of your knee, and moving your knee and leg from full extension to flexion. If there is a popping or snapping sensation, pain, or a feeling of tendons rubbing against each other, you probably have this form of bursitis.

You may also have an inflammation of the covering of the joint about the inner aspect or even outer aspect of the knee. This is called synovitis. It is difficult to differentiate synovitis from pes bursitis and, in fact, both may occur at once. The cause is the same, overpronation of the foot, and the treatment is likewise the same.

If you still have pain on the inside of the knee, and both you and your doctor are pretty sure that it is not the medial cartilage or the pes, then you could have an injury of a medial collateral ligament. The ligaments on the inside of the knee can be damaged or strained in the same manner as the ligaments on the outside. Usually, running itself will not damage these ligaments, but an old injury could begin to hurt again during running. If this is the case, consult an orthopedist.

I should mention that runners can have knee problems for

medical reasons. It is possible, for instance, to have gout or rheumatoid arthritis which flares up only when you run. If there is a family history of arthritis, you may have it. If your father had gout, there is a chance you have gout and that running will aggravate it. For this reason, any knee problem which does not respond soon to conventional treatment should be followed with laboratory tests to rule out any systemic disease.

BACK OF KNEE PAIN

Pain in the back of the runner's knee is most often caused by strains of the muscles in that area. The hamstrings are easily strained, as is the gastrocnemius muscle. Or people may think there is something wrong with the knee joint when, in fact, they have tendinitis resulting from running too fast or from applying too much strain on these structures.

The hamstrings are the muscles running down the back of the thighs. They tend to get very tight in long-distance runners. When the runner takes a longer stride, he may strain the muscles or tendons.

A good way to take care of hamstring injuries is to prevent them from happening in the first place. Preventive strengthening and stretching exercises are necessary. For strength, the athlete lies on his stomach and places a five-to-ten-pound weight on the back of the heel, then flexes and extends the knee (*fig. 19*). A good way to stretch the hamstrings is to do the hurdler's stretch—sitting on the ground and leaning forward, trying to touch the toes. Stretch the hamstrings also by placing the heel on a bench, starting with the knee bent and then slowly extending the knee to a straight position (*fig. 19*). Leaning forward places stress on the hamstrings.

It is not uncommon for runners to pull the gastrocnemius or calf muscle at knee-joint level or even above the knee joint where the tendons of the muscle have their origin. This is quite often secondary to running much faster than the athlete is accustomed to or running uphill.

There can be an even more serious problem in the back of the knee. This is called Baker's cyst, a defect in the capsule of the knee joint. It allows the capsule to bulge at the posterior aspect.

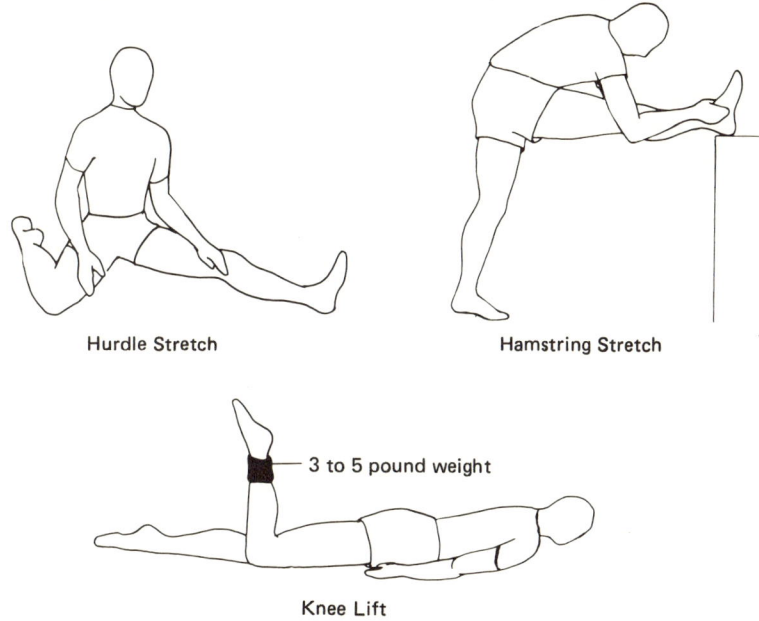

Hurdle Stretch   Hamstring Stretch

3 to 5 pound weight

Knee Lift

Figure 19
Hamstring Exercises

Thus, there is a squishy mass in the back of the knee. An orthopedist should be consulted for this. He may suggest various types of treatment, ranging from injection into the cyst to surgical excision.

Pain in the back of the knee may also be due to previous damage in some contact sport, leading to instability of the knee joint itself. X-rays are often helpful in diagnosing these knee problems. They are most valuable when looking for arthritis or bony damage. Another worthwhile test for difficult problems is an arthrogram in which dye is placed in the knee to look for cartilage defects. If you have been through the conservative route, have orthotics, have been checked out by a sports podiatrist and still have knee problems, something apparently is wrong with the inner aspect of the knee. If after an orthopedist has done X-rays and arthrograms, he still feels there is a problem with the cartilage in the knee, then an arthroscope may be necessary. Here, the doctor looks at the cartilage inside the knee with a special scope before surgery is considered.

6

Achilles Tendon Injuries

Darryl Hamerton is a physical therapist, with an excellent working knowledge of the body as a whole and how to rehabilitate the injured body. He spends his whole day treating athletes and other patients with severe injuries, but he has trouble taking care of himself.

When Darryl, then 38 years old, first came to see me, he was injured. He complained that his right Achilles tendon had been extremely painful off and on for the past eight years. Sometimes, there was even numbness around the tendon. He said that if he stopped running for a week, the pain would go away. He would use ultrasound, ice massage, and stretch, but the cures were never permanent. He related his recent history to me as follows:

He had run the West Valley Marathon. His right knee started hurting because his Achilles hurt and he had to change his running style. He ran for another month with pain, stopped running for three weeks because his Achilles hurt too much, then increased his mileage to five a day before the pain slowed him again. He tried heel lifts and ran for three days. The pain was so sharp that he changed his running style and put all the weight on the ball of his foot. This caused pain there, and he had to stop running.

Hamerton ran the Bay to Breakers, but the Achilles tendon became even more inflamed and tender to the touch. Now, he had trouble walking.

I asked him the usual questions about his past medical history, childhood diseases, etcetera. I was looking for clues that might suggest a family history of tendon problems, arthritis, or systemic disease which might affect tendons, joints, or bones. There were no such clues.

I examined Darryl and found that the sheath around the Achilles tendon was extremely inflamed, tight, and knotty. The tendon felt warmer on the injured side than on the opposite side. The thickness of the tendon was somewhat greater on the injured side than the other. On the uninjured side, flexibility at the ankle joint appeared normal, while it was limited on the right. When I moved the foot up and down, extending and flexing the ankle joint, there was crepitation or a sandpaperlike feeling around the tendon.

Biomechanically, Darryl had a Morton's foot with a moderate amount of overpronation due to a hypermobile first metatarsal and forefoot varus. In other words, the area under the first metatarsal and great toe did not touch the ground when the heel was perpendicular to the ground or the foot was essentially neutral. This meant that the foot had to collapse or roll in to bring itself to the ground. This pronation caused a torque on the Achilles tendon.

Further evaluation showed that Darryl had a right leg three-eighths inch shorter than the left. I assumed that he might be overstriding on the short right leg to catch up with the left leg. This overstriding caused him to land farther back on his right heel, and, as his foot slapped down, there might have been more torque on the Achilles. Overstriding also caused the foot to land forward of the center of gravity, making the ground push the body back. This push-back phenomenon forced the right foot and leg to absorb more stress. The stress not absorbed by bones or by the opening and closing of joints in the foot was absorbed by the muscles and tendons. In this case, the Achilles tendon was affected.

We were faced with an eight-year-old injury of the Achilles which had never really responded to rest, ultrasound, ice massage, or stretching. We were faced with an obvious inflammation and thickening of the sheath of the tendon. What I did not know was the condition of the tendon beneath the sheath. Was

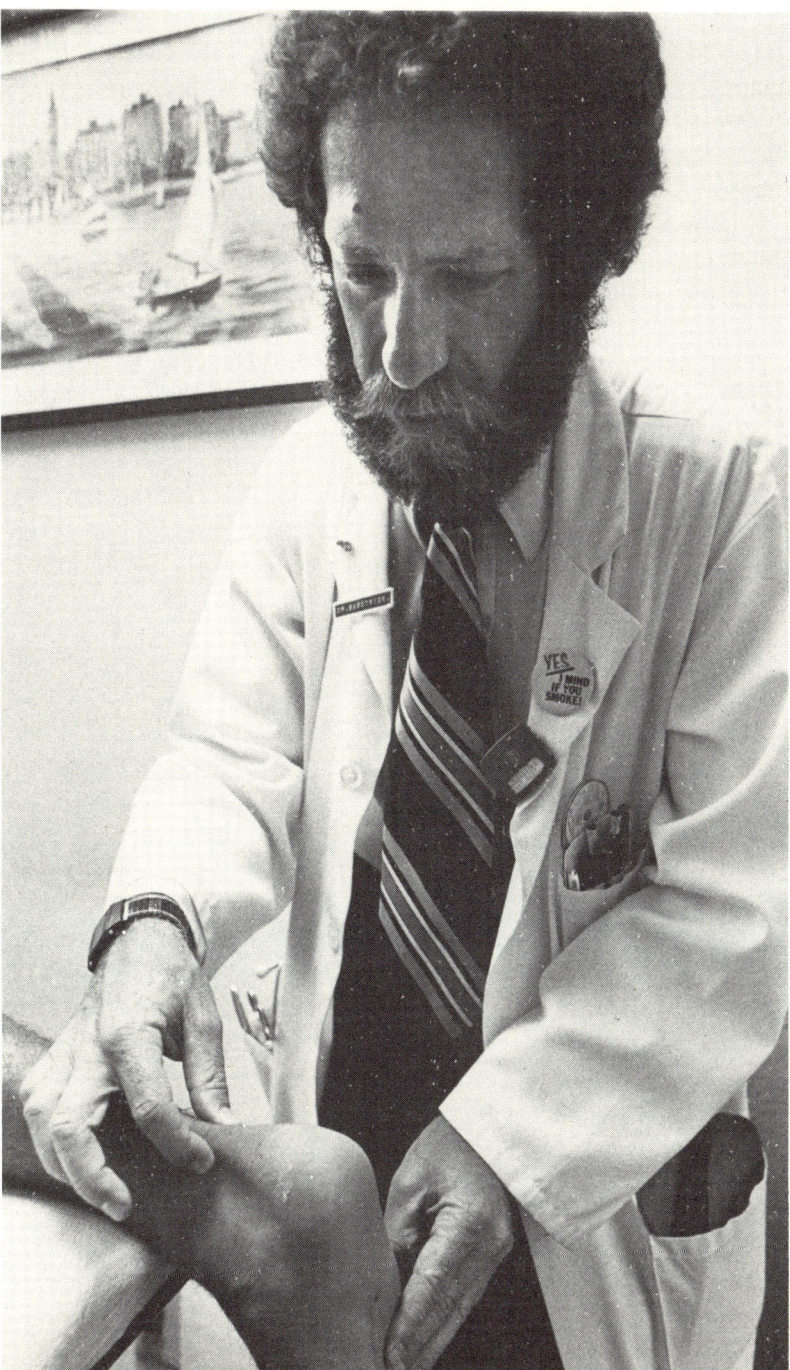

it perfectly normal, or was there degeneration of the tendon? Had there been any microtears of the tendon itself?

X-rays were taken and showed that the back of Hamerton's heel was somewhat enlarged and appeared to be rubbing on the tendon itself. There was, however, no calcification or bone formation affecting the Achilles tendon itself. Lab tests were taken, and they ruled out diseases such as gout and rheumatoid arthritis which occasionally go hand-in-hand with acute tendinitis.

I reviewed with Darryl all I knew about the Achilles tendon. because I felt it was important for both of us to know where we stood. I told him that the best treatment for acute tendinitis was rest for three to six weeks, quarter inch felt heel lifts, orthotics to help control the abnormal motions of the foot, as well as a physical therapy program including stretching and six minutes of ice massage after each gentle workout. I told him I was somewhat concerned about the condition of the tendon sheath and about the tendon itself.

With repeated damage to an Achilles, the inflammation itself sometimes causes deposits of scar tissue, and this might not respond to anti-inflammatory medications, ultrasound, ice, or stretching. In fact, surgery must be resorted to in some cases to remove the scar tissue. At this time, the Achilles tendon must be inspected. If it is white, glistening, and smooth, it is considered normal. If it is yellow or somewhat degenerated in appearance, it is a diseased tendon. When this occurs, it is necessary to make incisions into the tendon so that the healthy fat surrounding it can migrate to the tendon and the fat cells can, through a process of metaplasia, change into healthy tendon cells. The tendon itself in adults has no cells capable of self-repair. Therefore, it is necessary for surgery to create the proper tissue healing. In this case, we use fat.

Hamerton didn't have this surgery immediately. We first treated him conservatively with immobilization in an Unna boot, a soft cast which allows some motion but basically restricts the ankle joint and rests the Achilles tendon. A heel lift was also added to this flexible cast. He was immobilized for two weeks. Then, he was allowed to use physical therapy but told not to run. Sporthotics were made for him.

Within two months, his Achilles tendon was improved considerably. He then returned to running. But as he increased his mileage, the pain returned. He resumed physical therapy, stopped running, and the pain subsided. He started running again, and the pain, inflammation, and tenderness returned once more. This sequence continued until finally Darryl and I decided surgery was necessary. I related to him that I had done about fifteen similar surgeries, and the results to date had been quite good. One patient had won the Levi ride and tie contest once and had taken second another time.

Darryl's surgery was done in a hospital. The bump on the back of the heel was removed to take pressure off the Achilles. The sheath of the Achilles tendon was found to be quite thick and damaged, and it was released. The Achilles tendon itself was somewhat enlarged, yellow, and degenerated in appearance. Incisions were made into the tendon to allow for proper migration of surrounding fat.

Hamerton spent two weeks in a Jones cast, essentially half a cast with plaster only in the back from below the knee to the bottom of the foot. This cast immobilizes yet allows some motion so that stiffness does not occur. When the cast came off, Darryl began a stretching program and other physical therapy, and started to walk. He quickly went from walking to running, then slowly increased his mileage. His progress was extremely good.

When I last saw him, he was running five to six miles a day with no pain. He told me he is extremely pleased with the surgical results and has no hesitation to recommend it to other people in the same situation.

Do all Achilles problems need surgery? Of course not. Very few of them will ever need it. Most Achilles problems respond to stretching, ice, and a rational approach to training. But when you have had a problem for eight years, as Darryl Hamerton did, there is a good chance it may need surgery.

ACHILLES PAIN

If there is one tendon I would rather not treat, it is the Achilles. The reason is that it is a bit different from the other tendons athletes injure. The Achilles has a good blood supply to the sheath but a rather poor supply to the tendon itself. It is easily traumatized by shoes or objects rubbing against it, or by underlying bone. Most Achilles problems require rest, and no long-distance runner likes to rest. The Achilles is the connection between the calf muscles and the heel bone. The attached muscle group consists of the gastrocnemius, soleus, and a small, unused muscle called the plantaris. The three muscles together make up four-fifths of the bulk of the lower leg. Thus, the achilles tendon has an extremely heavy workload. It is responsible for stabilizing the knee at heel contact and for lifting the heel from the ground during propulsion. It functions then as a stabilizer and as a propelling muscle. The Achilles is a very important tendon, and when it is injured the runner is almost crippled.

Achilles tendons tend to mirror what is going on in the body. They have a good blood supply in younger people, but this supply diminishes as we age. Thus, the older a runner gets, the more dangerous it is for him to have an Achilles tendon problem.

Pain around the Achilles tendon can be due to a problem of the sheath, a problem of the tendon itself, or a combination of the two. Pain may come from a strain at the attachment of the tendon to the muscle or at the attachment of the tendon to the bone. (The Achilles anchors itself into the posterior one-third of the calcaneus. If a bump is present there, then this shelf of bone can actually rub or cut into the tendon, causing tendinitis.)

Tendinitis means inflammation of the tendon. Tenosynovitis or paratenonitis mean inflammation of the tendon sheath. There is a difference between the sheath of the Achilles and the sheath of other tendons. The Achilles has a loose, fatty sheath called the paratenon which has an exuberant blood supply and tends to move with the tendon like an accordion. Other tendons have a sheath more like a tube, and the tendon glides within this type. In both types of tendons, there is lubricating fluid between the tendon and sheath.

Let me explain step by step what can go wrong with the Achilles:

The most common Achilles problem is paratenonitis, or a strain of the loose, fatty tissue about the Achilles. It is usually secondary to overstress, and may be precipitated by running too fast or running hills. Stress can be cumulative and as it adds up can cause strain of the sheath. When this happens, there is usually some swelling about the Achilles along with pain. The swelling responds rather dramatically to abstinence from running. Also, a quarter-to half-inch felt heel lift helps the problem greatly.

Further treatment might consist of orthotics. This will help if there is excessive pronation of the foot, or even supination of the foot, causing strain on the Achilles sheath. A flat foot tends to have strain on the inside of the Achilles sheath, and a high-arched foot tends to have more strain on the outside of the sheath. Constant rolling from the outside to the inside of the foot can cause a strain of the whole Achilles tendon sheath.

Some patients have a dropped forefoot, called a forefoot equinus (*fig. 20*). If you have a relatively high arch when you are not standing on it, and the heel tends to be off the ground when the forefoot is touching the ground, you have this condition. The heel tends to sag down toward the ground when you run, and this places additional stress on the Achilles. A heel lift would help you. Place enough lift under the heel so there is no pain with walking. If pain still is there when you run, you may need even more lift. If even that doen't work, you need rest—at least two to three weeks of rest until there is no pain with walking. Riding a bike or swimming usually causes no pain with Achilles sheath problems, and is a good substitute while you heal.

Two aspirin a half-hour before running and using ice for six minutes after running are quite helpful. Running every other day is enough during the healing process. Cortisone injections are not a good idea for tendon sheath problems in the acute or initial phase. Chronic Achilles sheath problems, however, may need a cortisone injection, but I do this with reservation. I favor anti-inflammatory medication rather than an injection. The injections into the sheath are not harmful and may break up adhesions or scar tissue formation. But injections into the tendon itself can weaken it and could lead to a rupture.

Suppose you have a sore achilles that came on from racing and it does not appear to be responding to the treatments I've named. You may have severe tenosynovitis. There may be actual adhesions between the sheath and the Achilles itself. As

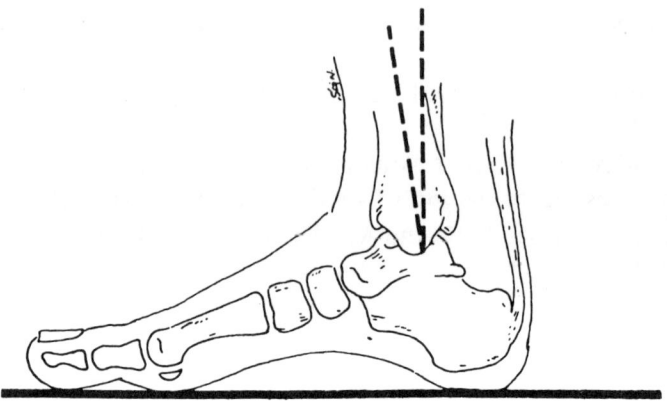

Neutral Foot

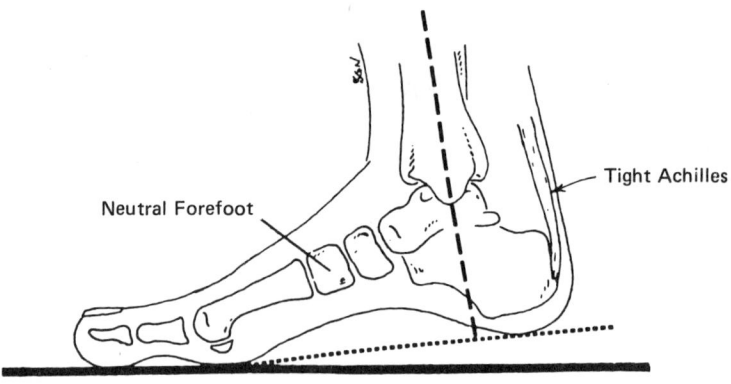

Neutral Forefoot

Tight Achilles

Normal Dorsiflexion

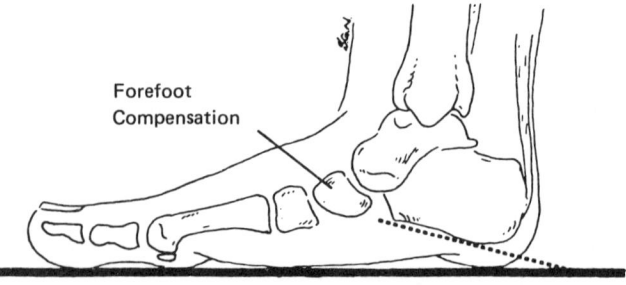

Forefoot
Compensation

Abnormal Dorsiflexion

Figure 20
Equinus Deformity

the Achilles tries to move through the sheath, there is a sandpaper sensation called crepitation. This condition requires immediate rest.

When my patients have this problem, there is no difficulty making the diagnosis. They come limping into the office, barely able to walk. When I have them stand on the ball of the foot, there appears to be adequate strength in the achilles and I can feel no tear of the tendon itself. But there is crepitation and a great deal of pain with motion of the foot up and down at the ankle joint when the achilles is stressed. Swelling of the sheath is obvious.

My treatment for this problem is immobilization in a soft cast for two weeks. I tell the athlete if we do not treat him this way, there is a good chance that surgery may be the end result. He may ride a bike or do other exercises during the healing phase. After two weeks of immobilization, felt heel lifts and orthotics are used to help ease the gradual return to walking and running.

If the runner continues to ignore the pain of tenosynovitis, there may be enough inflammation to cause some degeneration of the underlying tendon. This could become damaged and then rupture.

Suppose you have had what appeared to be a tendon sheath problem, it has been four weeks since the injury and you are getting better—but the tendon is still grossly swollen. You may have torn some fibers in the tendon itself. This is called tendinosis—a dangerous problem because it can advance to complete rupture or tear of the tendon. The best thing to do with tendinosis is to return to running slowly, and go on a stretching and weight program to strengthen the achilles tendon (*fig. 21*). When there is damage to the tendon itself, cortisone injections must be avoided.

The examining podiatrist can usually feel a little tear in the achilles tendon. Orthotics with heel lifts should be used. I suggest one-eighth-inch lifts for the remainder of the running career when there has been a tear of the achilles tendon. Special X-rays called xerograms may be helpful in making the diagnosis of an achilles tear or rupture.

There can be tendinosis without previous symptoms. In fact,

Figure 21
Achilles Stretch

if the runner has atherosclerosis, he can also have degeneration of the achilles tendon. He may step off a curb and suddenly rupture the achilles. What could be happening is a generalized degenerative process occurring in the body, with hardening of the arteries and increased cholesterol which causes some deterioration of the achilles tendon. Laboratory tests are often helpful in making this diagnosis if the runner shows a high cholesterol reading.

An achilles tendon rupture is a rather drastic event. The athlete cannot rise on the ball of the foot because he has lost all use of the calf muscles. There are two ways to treat this problem: A surgical approach assures proper healing of the ruptured achilles. But if one does not want surgery, then a cast must be worn for 12 weeks; for the first two weeks, the cast must be above the knee. I have treated achilles ruptures both ways and had success both ways. I tend to favor the surgical approach for athletic patients and the nonsurgical approach for sedentary patients.

Other achilles problems can occur where the tendon attaches to the heel bone. When this is the case, my initial treatment is to use foot orthotics to help stabilize the heel bone and minimize rubbing of bone on the tendon. If this does not work, then surgery may be performed to remove the bone underneath the achilles.

A strain of the achilles tendon where it attaches to the muscle takes time and patience to resolve. Besides reducing training, a heel lift is initially used as well as anti-inflammatory medication. With strengthening and flexibility exercises, these problems almost always resolve satisfactorily.

Runners who have had repeated bouts of achilles tendinitis or paratenonitis may not respond to conservative treatment due to adhesions and degeneration of the achilles tendon sheath. When this is the case, I have had very good results with surgically repairing the sheath. This is usually done under local anesthesia, and the athlete is back running in one to two months following surgery.

On occasion, I have operated on runners for what I thought was paratenonitis. They actually had a combination of tendon sheath problems and degeneration of the tendon itself. When this was the case, I made longitudinal incisions into the tendon so the fatty tissue surrounding it could migrate into the tendon and help heal it. The achilles tendon of a child can repair itself, but there is no way an adult tendon can do this. Therefore, in an adult we use the active cells from the surrounding fat to help in the healing.

Guidelines for achilles problems are as follows:

1. Cut way back on training.
2. No racing or hill running.
3. Two aspirin a half-hour before running, and six minutes of ice following running.
4. Stretch before running, after running, and, if there is pain during the run, stop and stretch then.
5. Use heel lifts, enough to eliminate pain.
6. If pain worsens with running, stop; you are inviting disaster.
7. If these do not work, see a podiatrist.

Finally, some achilles problems, particularly in young or small runners, may be secondary to stiff shoes. These runners work too hard trying to bend the shoe at the ball of the foot. If this is the case, simply slit the bottom of the shoe with three parallel lines across the ball so it flexes easier—or get new shoes with more flexibility.

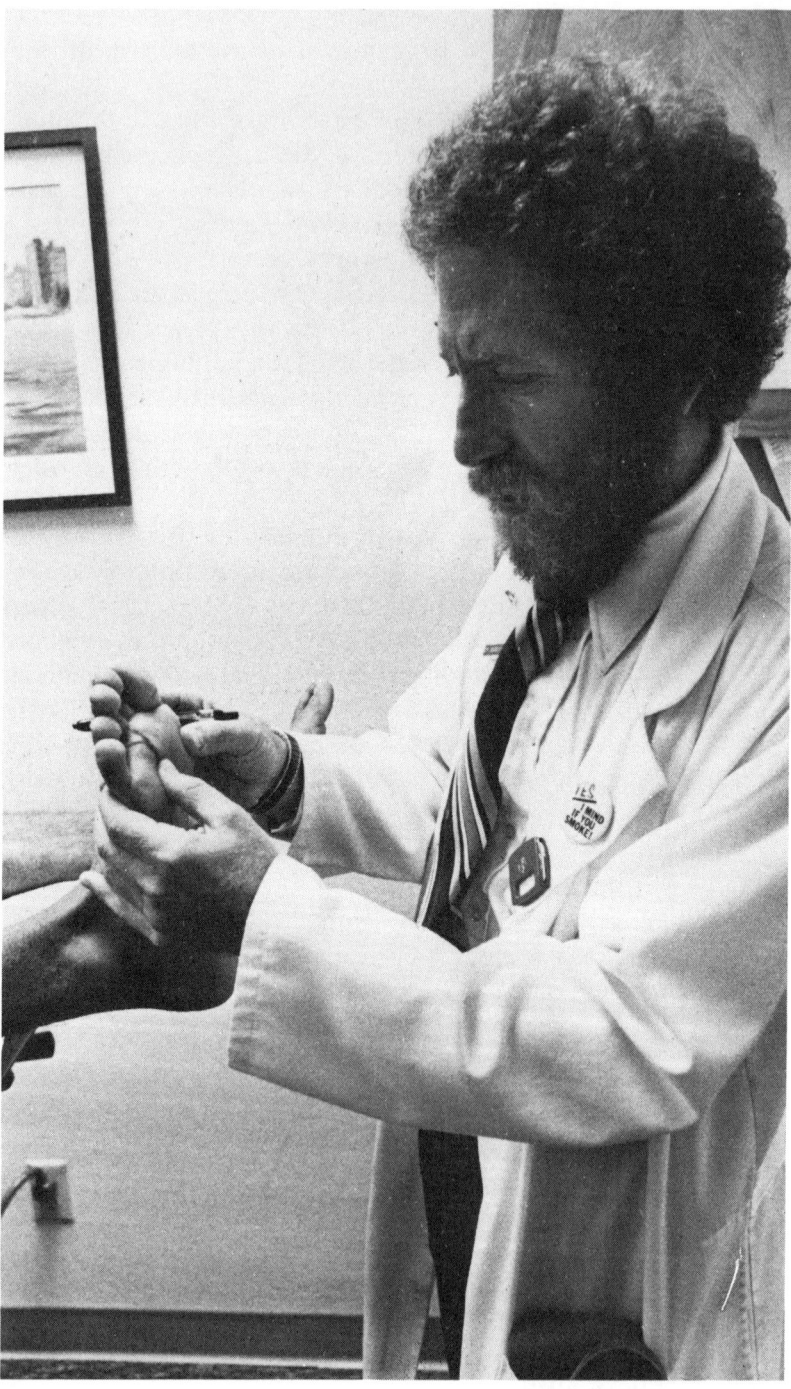

7

Nerve Injuries (Neuromas)

Sam Wilson, 42, had been running 30 miles weekly for the past couple of years. He then increased his mileage gradually to get ready for a marathon. He planned to reach 65 to 70 miles a week before the race.

Sam noticed a numbness on the ball of the foot which finally became aching pain. He would have sharp, shooting pains going to the bottoms of the third and fourth toes. At first, this pain did not bother him during his everyday activities but occurred at three or four miles when running. The pain then got worse and made the remainder of his run uncomfortable and difficult. As his mileage increased, the pain became severe enough to bother him during walking, and he began to dread his running since he could only go one or two blocks before the pain began. He wondered about a stress fracture or some form of tendinitis when he consulted me.

Upon examination, I did not see the usual swelling present with a stress fracture. I had him jump up and down on the ball of his foot, but the pain was not present. I checked all the tendons and soft-tissue structures going into the foot, and they all seemed fine—except for the plantar nerve which goes to the third and fourth toes. When I rubbed my fingers between the third and fourth metatarsal heads, there was a clicking mass in the space between these structures.

I then compressed the metatarsal heads together, and Sam experienced the same type of pain that he had when running. I placed my fingers over the nerve branches going to the bottoms of the third and fourth toes, and noted that these appeared to be somewhat enlarged. When I pricked the toes with a pin, sensation was decreased and, indeed, there was some numbness in the toes. X-rays showed some spreading of the third and fourth toes, which might occur if a soft-tissue mass was present. The bones appeared within normal limits, and there was no sign of stress fracture, also no sign of arthritis.

I made a tentative diagnosis of a plantar neuroma, also called Morton's interdigital neuroma.

I explained to Wilson that it was entirely possible the increased mileage caused enough pressure on this nerve, by rubbing from the bone and by rubbing from the tight band of tissue that joins the metatarsal heads together, to cause damage to the nerve sheath and thus the nervelike pain when running. I also told him that it is common for there to be a combination of a neuroma and some bursitis, which is a deep blister, or even tendinitis.

Approximately 60 to 70 percent of my patients whom I suspect to have neuromas respond favorably to nonoperative procedures. This includes injections of a long- and short-acting cortisone with some vitamin B_{12} to shrink the inflammation around the nerve sheath, so the nerve can work its way loose from any adhesions or traumatic scar tissue which may be present.

I explained to Sam that one and sometimes two injections are necessary, and that in rare instances I will use three injections. I also explained that there can be some soreness from these injections which may last anywhere from a couple of hours to six days, but following this the results are good enough to make up for the soreness or inconvenience from the injection. This type of cortisone injection, when it is used with a total rehabilitative program, is safe and does not cause any permanent damage to the adrenal gland or to the body itself. Likewise, if it is not going into the joint, there is no problem with a drug-induced arthritis.

In cases such as Wilson's with a Morton's-type foot and hypermobility of the foot, it is good to stabilize the foot with an orthotic. At first, we use a soft, temporary support to make sure the patient is a candidate for orthotics. I put a neuroma pad on the orthotics to spread the metatarsal heads apart. This works in most cases, but at times this pad can irritate the nerve and must be removed. If the pad works well, when I make permanent orthotics I also place a neuroma bubble on them to spread the metatarsal heads.

One injection gave Wilson dramatic relief. When he came back one week later for his follow-up visit, he told me that within a day he was able to run and was gradually increasing his mileage, training for a marathon again. He also told me that he had less fatigue when using the soft supports and that the neuroma pad helped. This being the case, I casted Sam for more permanent orthotics with a neuroma bubble. It was unnecessary to give a second injection, because he was asymptomatic.

Sam returned three weeks later to pick up his permanent orthotics. Some of the pain had returned. I elected to use another cortisone injection. When he came back four weeks later, he was totally symptom-free. One month after that, he was still doing just fine.

NEUROMA PAIN

Neuromas can occur anywhere that a nerve is traumatized but are most commonly found on the forefoot between the metatarsals, where the toes join the metatarsals (*fig. 22*). This usually occurs in the third interspace, between the third and fourth toes. It is very rare in the fourth interspace, not too common in the second interspace and can occur frequently in the first interspace.

For some reason, abnormal motion of the foot or abnormal trauma causes irritation to the nerve, and the nerve sheath gets larger. Picture an electrical wire with insulation around it. Well, the insulation in this case gets too big due to the trauma. The nerve responds to excessive pressure or stress by trying to form a protective covering. This leads to overgrowth and causes the neuroma. Along with this, excessive motion may cause a bit of inflammation about the nerve. This is called chronic fibrosis if it becomes firm and gristlelike. A bursa can also form in association with a neuroma.

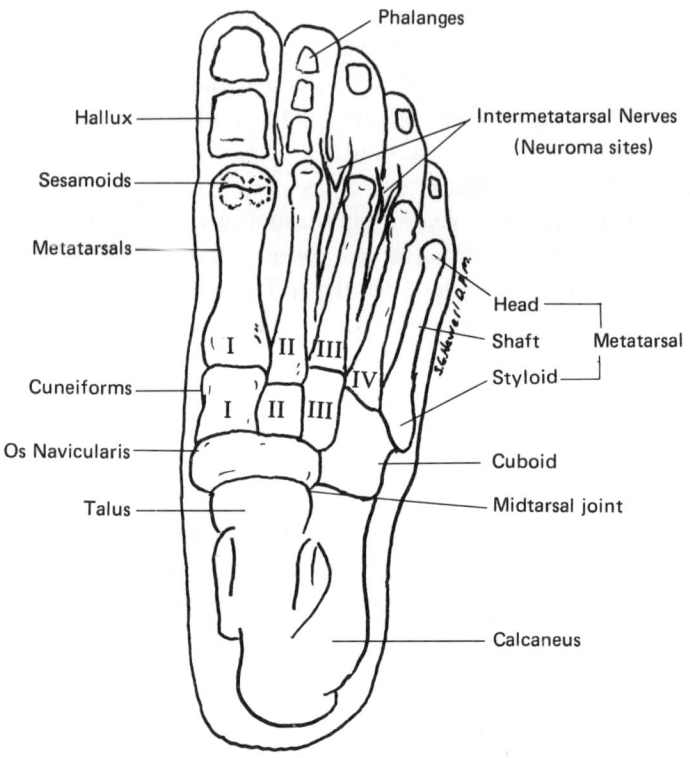

Figure 22
Interdigital Neuroma

The first symptom is a dull ache. With distance runners, it usually is associated with a certain amount of mileage. It may begin after running six miles, when a burning sensation in the foot is noted. After a while, the foot itself may become numb. The numbness is usually in adjacent toes, because the nerve feeds the bottom of one toe and the same area on the adjacent toe. Thus, a Morton's neuroma of the third interspace might give numbness on the bottoms of the third and fourth toes, the ones fed by this nerve.

If you press in the interspace with your finger, this may cause electric-like pain. Some runners have so much pain that they have to take off their shoes and massage their feet to make it go away. Because the pain is caused by irritation on the nerve, it can radiate along the course of the nerve, and shoot from the ball of the foot all the way back to the heel and sometimes up the inner aspect of the leg.

What can you do if you have a neuroma? The burning pain usually causes enough concern and discomfort that you will seek the attention of a podiatrist. I usually tell my patients to get wider shoes so that the bones are not pressing on the nerve. (Long-distance bike riders who wear tight-fitting Italian shoes come into the office with neuroma-type pain, and simply getting wider shoes takes care of the problem.)

I evaluate the foot to see if some type of orthotic might be helpful, and I often use a neuroma pad on the bottom of the foot to spread the metatarsal heads apart. Quarter-inch felt cut in the shape of a triangle works nicely. X-rays are taken to rule out other causes of pain in the foot such as stress fractures, arthritis or bony spurs.

Initial treatment consists of a mixed cortisone injection to shrink the swelling around the sheath of the nerve. At times, vitamin B_{12} may help the nerve restore itself to a healthy attitude. If the injections do not work, orthotics do not work, and rest does not work, then surgery is the treatment of choice. Surgery can easily be done under local anesthesia, and the runner is usually only off of running for three to six weeks. Following surgery, there will be some numbness where the nerve used to be. This is a sensory nerve and there will be no weakness from loss of motor function, since the nerve does not go to any muscles in this area of the foot. The incision is made on the top of the foot thus avoiding the possibility of pain from a scar on the bottom of the foot.

8

Heel Injuries

I first met Mark Olsen in 1977, but had heard from him earlier when he wrote me a letter describing very high-arched feet which absorbed shock poorly and caused a great deal of pain in his legs and ankles when he ran. I had referred him to a podiatrist in his hometown who had treated him for this problem.

When Mark came to me, he was complaining of pain under the heel of his right foot. The pain was localized where the thin skin meets the thick skin under the inside ankle bone. During running, this pain became almost unbearable. There also was pain in the plantarfascia, the tissue immediately beneath the skin and fat which runs from the heel bone to the metatarsal heads.

I sat Mark down in a chair and moved his great toe toward his head. The plantarfascia became tight. When the great toe was relaxed, the plantarfascia loosened somewhat but remained tighter than normal. Mark had a dropped forefoot, or forefoot equinus. The ball of his foot was lower than the heel. His extremely high-arched foot was evident when he stood up.

There was pain over the medial plantarfascia where it attached to the heel bone. I lubricated the skin and palpated with my fingers over the various branches of the posterior tibial nerve behind the inside ankle bone. This nerve, which runs straight down from the ankle bone into the bottom of the foot, appeared to be bound down with scar tissue. There was pain when I palpated this nerve, and there also was clicking sensation under my fingers. There appeared to be a mass under the heel similar to a stone bruise.

X-rays were taken of the foot and showed no heel spur. However, the X-rays showed Olsen did have an extremely high arch, and there was some excessive bone under the heel bone immediately beneath the nerve. My diagnosis was chronic plantarfasciitis as well as entrapment of the medial calcaneal nerve. It also appeared as though he had excessive bone on the medial condyle of the calcaneus.

Mark had previously been treated with Sporthotic devices which were made by another podiatrist, and he appeared to be functioning well. Despite this, his foot still hurt. This was not the fault of the Sporthotics but the fault of the foot itself. Too much damage had been done to be reversed by Sporthotics alone. I explained this to him and told him that, since he had cortisone and various forms of physical therapy in the past, surgery appeared to be our next step.

I would release the plantarfascia surgically and also check the medial calcaneal nerve. If the nerve was damaged or entrapped, as I felt it was, release or resection would be necessary. This could cause mild patchy numbness in the heel of the foot but would not affect any muscles since this is a sensory, not a motor, nerve. I also told him I would look at the bottom of the bone of the heel. If it appeared to be rough or a trouble spot, I would rasp it smooth.

Mark agreed with my surgical plans, and the surgery was carried out under local anesthesia. I made him wear a Jones cast, with plaster only in the back of the leg and foot, for about three weeks to help stretch out the plantarfascia while it was healing.

Olsen's post-operative course was uneventful. Within three weeks after the cast was removed, he was walking and running without pain. He was elated! He lived in Minnesota but called me long-distance almost every day to tell me how he was doing.

About two months after he had surgery and was running well, he called up complaining of similar pain in the opposite foot. I recalled then that he had mentioned mild pain there when he first saw me, but I assumed that the Sporthotics and proper stretching exercises would take care of this problem. They did not.

Approximately six months after the original surgery, Mark returned to my office to have the other foot operated on. He told me that even if the foot did not hurt, he would still have the surgery because the plantarfascia release gave his foot so much flexibility and improved his running form to a great extent.

This is not an isolated case. In fact, I have performed plantarfascial releases in several patients who have a high-arched foot and tight plantarfascia. Following the surgical release, there is increased flexibility of the foot and the foot functions better during running.

I mention Mark Olsen's case because it has a happy ending. It also has a lesson to teach. If a runner is unwilling to change his sport and become a bicycle rider or swimmer, if he has his heart set on running, he may sometime have to consider a surgical procedure to change his foot. Mark made this decision and had good results.

BOTTOM OF HEEL PAIN

Pain on the bottom of the heel, plantar heel pain, in runners can have a number of causes. There can be an acute traumatic injury, a chronic overuse injury which gradually worsens, or arthritic conditions such as gout or rheumatoid arthritis. We can divide the problems into those affecting soft tissue and those involving bone.

Soft-tissue injuries include stone bruises; strains of the ligaments, fascia, or muscles which attach to the bottom of the heel; and heel neuromas. The runner also might have a callus or seed corn on the heel, which is quite painful. Warts are often present.

The important precaution with any heel problem, soft-tissue or bony, is to protect the heel adequately and guard against impact shock. Softer surfaces naturally are easier on the heel than harder surfaces, and shoes with good shock-absorbing properties are essential. Sponge-rubber heel cups or pads are also useful. If there is abnormal pronation or contact with the heel, then an orthotic will help. High-arched feet may need an eighth-inch heel lift.

Heel neuromas are quite common. A branch of the medial calcaneal nerve comes off the posterior tibial nerve at the inside ankle bone. This nerve divides into three main branches. The medial calcaneal branch then gives off four or five smaller branches which pierce the deep tissue, then become superficial and lie in the fat. They may get entrapped in the thick tissue at the bottom of the heel where the pain occurs. It radiates and is out of proportion to what is really wrong because the the nerve is involved. You can usually rub your fingers over the nerve and feel a clicking sensation with radiating pain.

When a heel neuroma is present, I try orthotics, padding and injections of long- and slow-acting cortisone along the course of the nerve to shrink inflammation, and use lidocaine to free the nerve from entrapment. If cortisone injections, orthotics, rest, and softer shoes do not work, then surgery is indicated. It involves the relatively simple removal of the entrapped portion of nerve.

The other main soft-tissue problem is runner's bump on the bottom of the heel, commonly called a stone bruise. This can indeed come from stepping on a stone, although that is not the only cause. When there is a lot of pounding on the heel, a sac forms to help protect the heel bone. This bursa can become inflamed, and bursitis can result. Often, a stone bruise is associated with bursitis. When this is the case, there is a mushy or clicky feeling on the bottom of the heel, which can be quite painful. Aspirin often helps, along with accommodative heel pads and orthotics. Cortisone injections into the bursa tend to shrink it and allow the walls of the bursa to collapse. Very rarely, the bursa has to be excised surgically.

Older patients may have lost a lot of the sponginess in the plantar fat pad of the heel, a condition that may be accentuated by diseases such as rheumatoid arthritis. When this happens, they need an orthotic with a great amount of material to absorb shock in the heel.

Many runners develop problems at the attachment of the plantarfascia to the plantar shelf of the heel (*fig. 23*). You can find your plantarfascia by rising on the ball of your foot. It is

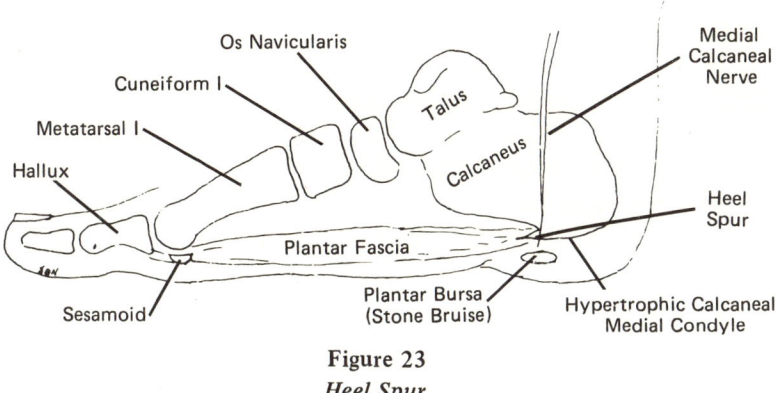

Figure 23
Heel Spur

the band of tissue under the arch. This has three strips—the medial, central, and lateral. The medial strip is the most common injury site.

Plantarfasciitis can be felt either in the arch or at the attachment of the plantarfascia to the bottom of the heel. A chronic pulling of the plantarfascia can cause a heel spur. The plantarfascia frequently is strained when the running is on the ball of the foot, and runners with high-arched feet are predisposed to this ailment.

The treatment for plantarfasciitis is to rest it by slowing down and running less on the ball of the foot. If there is too much pronation, then foot orthotics are necessary. For acute problems, rest, taping, and aspirin are the treatments of choice. For chronic problems, those that have been present for two to three weeks, a cortisone injection may be necessary to break up the scar tissue which probably has formed in an abnormal way, causing pain every time the scar tissue is stretched. Running every other day allows the runner to stretch out the plantarfascia and some of the scar tissue, but to avoid too much stress. Taping may be necessary for six to eight weeks to allow proper resting of the plantarfascia. Heel lifts help fasciitis associated with high-arched feet.

Plantarfasciitis can actually be caused by orthotics if they are too rigid. When I first dispensed orthotics for runners six to seven years ago, we mostly used the hard plastic type. We found that although other problems associated with overuse injuries

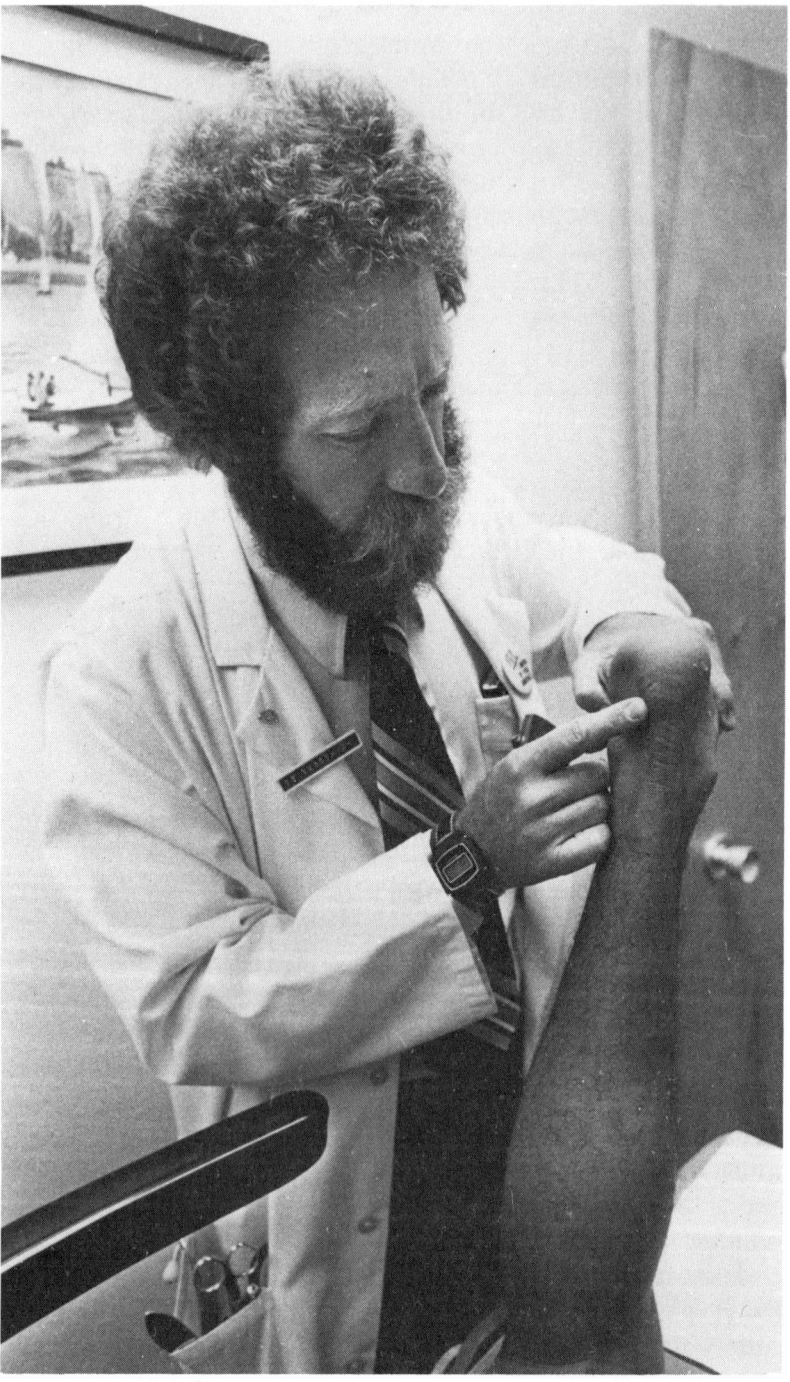

were corrected, some foot problems were aggravated. Runners who went faster than six minutes per mile and spent a great deal of time on the balls of their feet pressed the plantarfascia against the plastic and caused irritation. At times, orthotics will cause nodules to form on the plantarfascia, and these are very difficult to eliminate. For this reason, I tend to use a Sporthotic or flexible plastic device for patients susceptible to plantarfascial problems. When a more rigid orthotic is used, it needs to be heated and pushed down in the area of tenderness over the plantarfascia.

If conservative treatment does not work and somebody has a chronic problem lasting one to two years, then surgery may give good results. In this procedure, the plantarfascia is released from its attachment to the calcaneus so that it will heal in an elongated manner. This can be done under local anesthesia, and the runners usually is active again four to five weeks after surgery.

Along with plantarfasciitis, there can be pain in the heel area at the attachment of the short broad muscles, the abductor hallucis, which fills in the inner aspect of the arch to the heel bone. Strain of this muscle is very difficult to distinguish from a heel spur syndrome or plantarfasciitis, but it responds to the same type of treatment.

There may even be compression of the nerves in this area. The medial and lateral plantar nerves pass on top of the abductor hallucis muscle, and a tight abductor may press on the nerve, causing radiating pain into the arch and along the heel.

Bony problems include the heel spur syndrome, and stress fractures of the calcaneus itself or the growth plate called the calcaneal apophysis.

Heel spur syndrome is really a catch-all term which describes plantarfasciitis, myositis of the abductor hallucis and periostitis which occurs at the attachment of the muscles and fascia to the bone. There also can be pain from the spur itself. This spur is formed for mechanical reasons, usually excessive pronation or excessive pull in those who have a high-arched foot. The body responds to this by laying down more bone.

Heel spurs usually respond to the same type of treatment as plantarfasciitis: orthotics, taping, and rest. Heel cups also are useful. I incorporate the cup into the orthotic. This keeps the plantar fat underneath the heel and helps with plantar fat problems as well as heel spur injuries.

At times, there can be a problem of a bony nature under the medial condyle of the calcaneus. This is not really a heel spur problem but more a problem of an irregular surface on the bottom of the heel. This usually is associated with another soft-tissue problem such as bursitis or nerve entrapment. If orthotics do not work, some form of surgery is necessary.

Heel spurs also respond extremely well to surgery, as long as the proper diagnosis has been made and the surgeon is careful to look for any irregularities of the medial calcaneal nerve and to do a clean plantarfascial release. Following heel spur surgery, which can be done under local anesthesia, the athlete usually is running again in five to six weeks. I have had extremely good results with these surgeries to remove the spur, smooth down the bottom of the heel, and release the plantarfascia. Most athletes require orthotics after heel-spur surgery.

Younger athletes, ages 11 to 15, get stress fractures of the growth plates. The best treatment is six weeks of rest and soft foot supports. These fractures usually heal uneventfully, but if they recur the youngster should do no jumping for that season and, in fact, should avoid jumping until the growth plate has come together with the main body of the calcaneus. This usually occurs one or two years after the stress fracture.

Adults can get stress fractures, too. These were quite common in boot camp during the World War II, Korean, and Vietnam War eras. Usually, the calcaneus is unaccustomed to the stress being placed upon it, and it responds first with a generalized weakening of the bone in preparation to a strengthening. The problem is that the individual places additional stress on the heel during the weakened phase, and a crack occurs before the repair phase can take place. The treatment is six weeks of rest.

BACK OF HEEL PAIN

Pain in the back of the heel most often comes from runner's bumps, technically known as retrocalcaneal exostoses (*fig. 24*). These used to be known as pump bumps when I went to

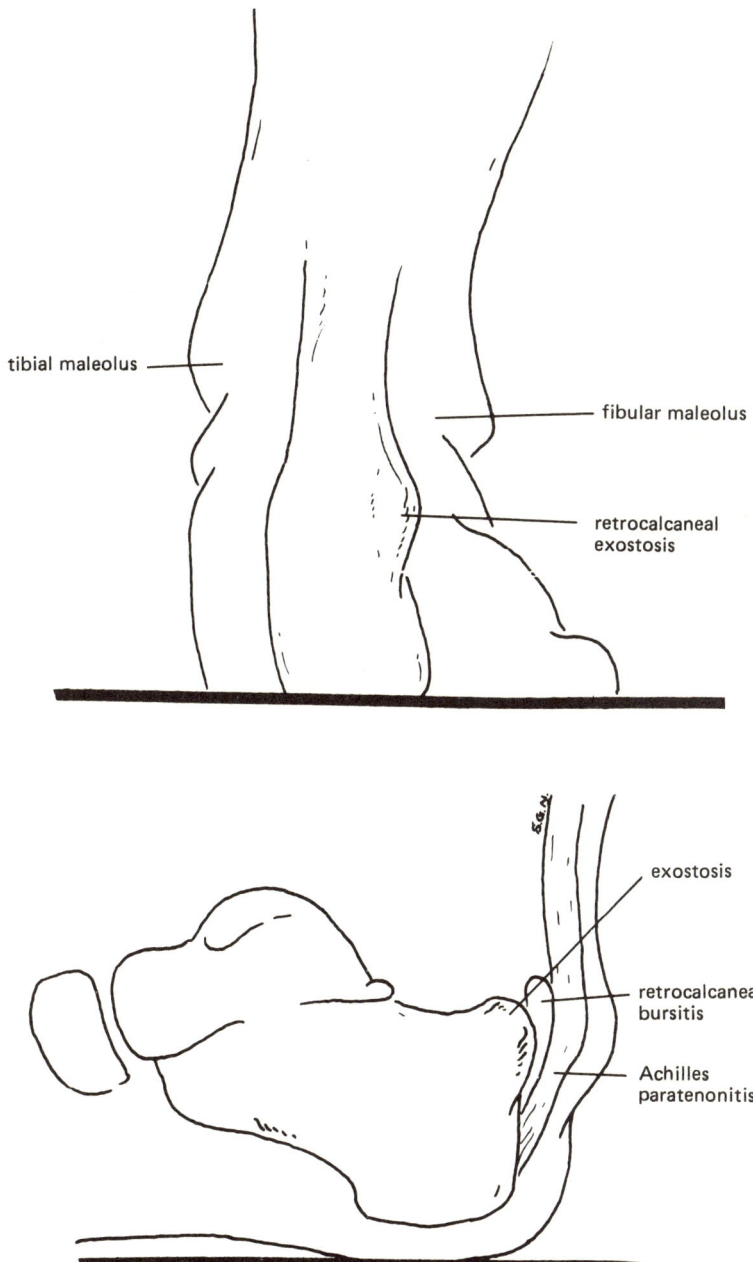

tibial maleolus

fibular maleolus

retrocalcaneal
exostosis

exostosis

retrocalcaneal
bursitis

Achilles
paratenonitis

Figure 24
Retrocalcaneal Exostosis

school, because girls would wear loafer shoes which would rub up and down on the heel and cause irritation over the back of the heel bone. This chronic irritation would often cause the bone to respond to the pressure with excessive growth, and a bony bump would form.

The same happens in runners if the heel moves too much in the shoe. Of course, a runner can also have a deformed calcaneus which becomes symptomatic when he places stress on it.

There is usually more pronation in running than in walking or standing, because the base of gait is zero in running whereas there usually is a wide stance in walking. This causes contact on the outside of the heel and excessive pronation. The outer, upper aspect of the heel then rubs in the shoe, and any protrusion of bone that is present causes irritation.

One serious complication is that the Achilles tendon inserts into the middle one-third of the back of the heel, and the calcaneus is underneath the Achilles. Thus, when the calcaneus goes through a rolling motion it can cause irritation to the Achilles. It can contribute to tendinitis, or a bursa can be formed between the bone and the tendon. If the tendon itself is forced to roll along with the bone, as usually happens, a bursa can form over the tendon along with tendinitis. This then becomes a runner's bump.

Pain in the heel bone also can be caused by nonathletic problems which become more symptomatic during sports activity. An example is arthritis of the heel. These cases are most troublesome, because one may treat them first as biomechanical problems with no improvement. I find it useful in nonresponsive heel pain to get blood tests to see if arthritis or gout is present. Infections and tumors of the heel are rare, but also can occur.

The first treatment for runner's bumps is to decrease the abnormal pronation with some form of foot orthotic or perhaps a shoe with a varus wedge. The next thing to do is take pressure off the bump. This can be done with one-fourth-inch felt or sponge rubber with a hole cut out where the bump is. This places pressure on the surrounding tissue instead of the bump. If the bump is inflamed or a bursa is present, consult a doctor to see if any additional treatment might be necessary.

When a youngster going through a growth spurt is involved,

and the growth plate is not fused to the main body of the calcaneus, he should be taken away from jumping sports or fast running until the active phase or immediate pain is gone. This may take two to four weeks. He then should have a soft orthotic made with about a quarter-inch heel lift to ease the stress on the back of the heel. If pain persists, the youngster should be told to find another sport for the season. It should be explained to him that it is ridiculous for him to keep injuring himself while he is growing rapidly. Sooner or later, flexibility will increase as his muscles and tendons increase in length to catch up with his bone growth.

An eighth- to quarter-inch heel lift of felt or sponge rubber also works well for older patients with runner's bumps.

Occasionally, bursitis in this area needs a cortisone injection. Before this is done, I suggest taking two aspirin a half-hour before running. Icing for six minutes after running and then deep massage also are helpful. The back of the shoe may be cut out and elastic put in its place to take pressure off of the achilles and bump.

If there is real deformity of the heel bone, then biomechanical treatment may not help. Surgery may be required. This is relatively simple and can be done under local anesthesia. The post-operative course is usually uneventful. The patient wears a splint or plaster cast over rolled cotton on the back of the leg and foot for approximately ten to fourteen days. This Jones cast offers compression and also helps to decrease excessive motion, especially where the achilles attaches to the heel bone, but allows some motion so that stiffness and loss of strength do not occur.

If you have a runner's bump, have tried all the conservative treatments available, and the bump is still painful enough to limit your running, I suggest you consult a sports podiatrist and consider some form of surgical relief.

9

Foot Injuries

Benton Hart's racing credentials included a 5000-meter time of 13:49 and a two-mile best of 8:29 while running for Brigham Young University and the West Valley Track Club.

Benton, then 22, came to my office in May 1978 with pain at the top of the mid-aspect of his foot. He told me he had every type of conservative treatment while in college, including immobilization of the foot in a plaster cast, four separate cortisone injections, ultrasound, orthotics, and anti-inflammatory medications. Despite this, he still hurt every time he got up on the ball of his foot or pronated his foot.

I examined Hart at length, and had him run up and down the hall, checking his stride and biomechanics. I noted that he tended to favor the sore foot, putting more weight on the opposite foot. He appeared to be jamming the talar navicular joint. We tried taping the foot and using soft, temporary orthotics. In later visists, he said this had done no good at all. I then told him that more permanent orthotics would be no help, either, since the temporary supports and taping had failed.

Upon reviewing the X-rays, I pointed out that it appeared jamming of the midtarsal joint was causing his pain. I had seen other distance runners and sprinters with this problem, and they had responded favorably to surgery which entailed removing excessive bone on the top of the foot to allow the midtarsal joint to function freely.

Benton's surgery was carried out under local anesthesia since he wished to go home after the surgery and had someone at home to take care of him. At the time of surgery, the midtarsal joint was explored, and it was found that Benton had an actual coalition. This means that, along with the jamming on top of the foot, there was extra bone in the midtarsal joint. A bar and loose piece of bone was found in the midtarsal joint, coming off the outside aspect of the navicular bone and jamming into the cuboid bone. This accounted for the pain when he had any motion of the foot. This is a rather rare finding, but the surrounding soft tissue showed inflammatory changes consistent with the chronic problem. The bar was excised from the midtarsal joint, which allowed for full motion.

When I last saw Hart, five months after surgery, he noted that he was running well on the ball of his foot and had no pain. He did, however, have a small problem. He had been training in distance flats and decided to run a race in his spiked shoes after doing no training in them for quite some time. He'd tied his spikes too tight and ended up with tendinitis on the foot that didn't have surgery. He returned to the office, hoping he did not have a coalition in that foot. I assured him he did not and told him with proper care the tendinitis would respond well.

Benton Hart's case describes a very difficult diagnosis and a problem that indeed will not respond to orthotics, medications, or injections. Benton had an injured foot that needed surgical repair. Surgery usually is the last resort for an athletic injury, but at times like this it is more conservative than the other treatment Hart had received.

About the same time I operated on Benton, one of his teammates, Paul Doughty, also came to my office with a painful foot. His pain was likewise occurring when he ran on the ball of his foot. He had a large protrusion called an os navicularis in the medial longitudinal arch of his foot. Apparently, he was running in a race and landed heavily on the ball of his foot, pulling the os navicularis loose from the main body of bone. This resulted in a nonhealing separation, and every time he overused his foot he had pain. Again, the only successful treatment for this kind of problem was surgery.

At the time of surgery, the excessive bone and fractured portion were removed. When last seen, approximately six weeks following the surgery, Paul was running well. I told him at the time that he could try doing a bit of speed work again.

BOTTOM OF FOOT PAIN

Pain on the bottom of the foot, like pain in the heel, can be divided into soft-tissue problems and those of the bony architecture of the foot. Since we have already discussed heel pain, this chapter concentrates on the arch, midfoot, ball of the foot, and the toes.

The midfoot or the arch can suffer chronic strain from overuse, or can have acute strain with a sudden twisting of the foot. Overuse injuries encompass plantarfasciitis (see chapter 8) as well as strains of the intrinsic muscles of the foot, those arising in the foot and inserting somewhere else in the foot. These muscles with a main function of stabilizing have a tendency to fatigue in an imbalanced foot. This in turn may cause the arch to become unstable.

We talked in chapter 2 about how forefoot varus (Morton's foot syndrome) and forefoot valgus create imbalances between the forefoot and the rearfoot. These biomechanical problems also cause overuse of the intrinsic muscles of the foot. The compensation in forefoot varus is usually pronation. This lowering of the arch stretches the muscles of the foot, especially in the medial longitudinal arch. A high-arched foot with a forefoot valgus tends to stretch the outer aspect of the foot, and the runner may feel like he has a sprained foot.

A sprain is an example of an acute injury. This may be a sprain of the talonavicular joint or medial longitudinal arch, or a sprain of a ligament in this area. Sprains of the inner aspect of the foot are common in jumping sports such as basketball and hurdling. There is usually pain right over the arch produced by motion of the foot between the talus and the navicular bones. Along with the sprain of the ligament, there may also be tendinitis along the posterior tibial tendon that helps hold up the arch.

Acute pain over the inner aspect of the arch, and especially over the protuberance called the os navicularis, may be the hint of something more serious than just an arch strain. X-rays are

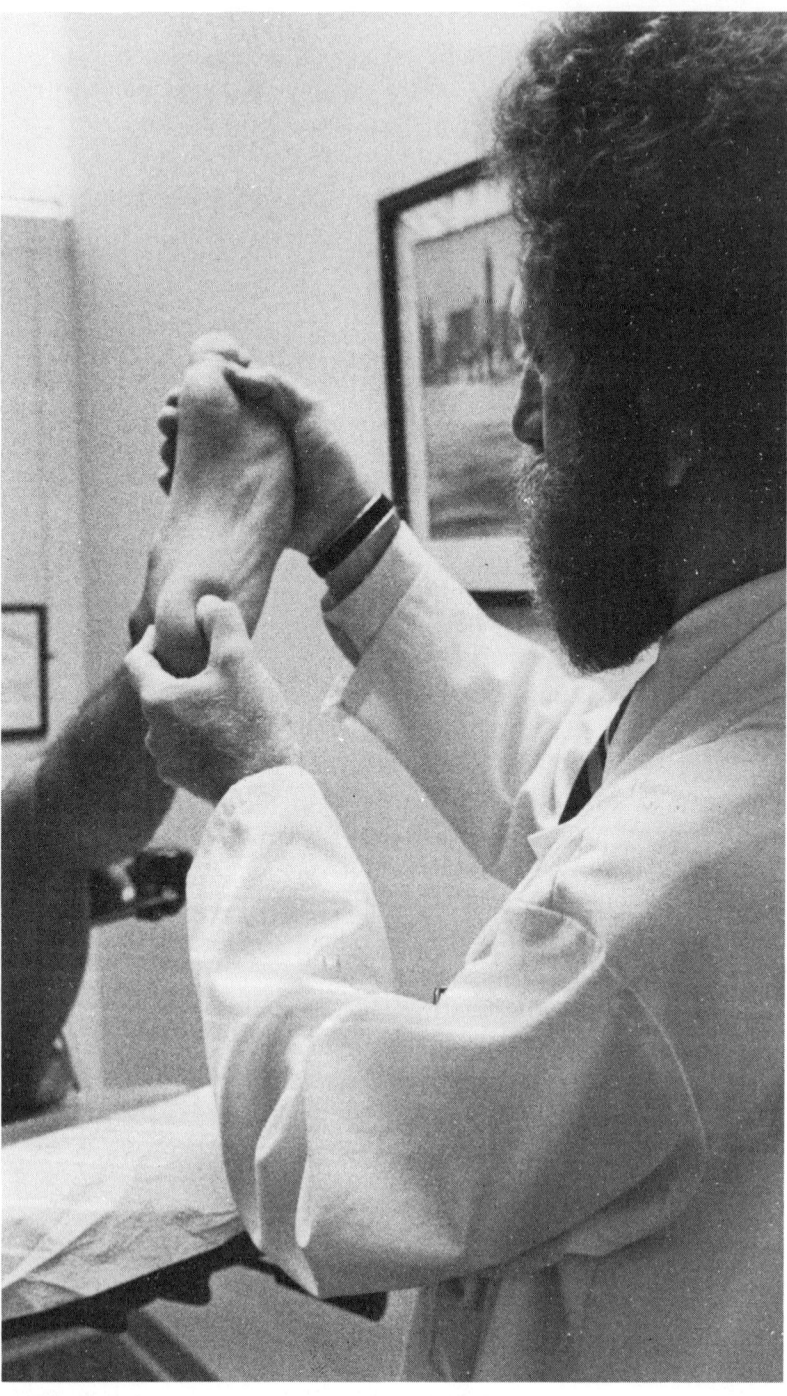

necessary to confirm a fracture or stress fracture. Rest is the treatment of choice, along with taping of the foot. Certainly, nothing should be done which aggravates the condition or causes pain. Pain of an acute nature on the outside of the foot could be a stress fracture of the cuboid bone, but more likely—especially with a high-arched foot or a forefoot valgus condition—it is a strain or sprain of the calcaneocuboid joint with minimal dislocation of the cuboid bone. At times, a podiatrist can put the cuboid bone back in place by inserting a pad underneath the cuboid and then taping the foot. Orthotic foot control usually prevents further subluxed cuboids.

With all strains of the arch, some form of taping to rest the arch and foot orthoses are indicated. If a fracture is present, a cast may be required for six to eight weeks to allow proper healing. Likewise, severe sprains may require immobilization if the athlete is not comfortable while walking with tape and an orthotic.

Exercises can be done to strengthen the arch and the broad muscles of the foot. These exercises consist of standing on the ball of the foot, jumping rope, and working on flexibility of the toes. A good exercise is to curl a towel under the foot with the toes (*fig. 25*). I also teach my patients to isolate various muscles in their feet so they know how to strengthen weakened muscles. This is very hard to explain in a book but can easily be demonstrated.

Runners can have various bony problems which are not fractures. The os navicularis syndrome is not uncommon; it causes problems in runners who get up on the balls of their feet. I have seen several young runners with os navicularis who have little difficulty in long, slow distance running but have a great deal of pain with sprinting. This is due to the tight-fitting track shoes and the amount of force placed on the foot during sprinting. A simple surgical procedure to remove the excessive bone in the medial longitudinal arch works quite well. The athlete is usually back running four to six weeks after this type of surgery.

Repeated sprains of the foot or arch may cause some damage to the styloid process of the fifth metatarsal. Likewise, a fracture may occur in this area with acute sprains of the ankle joint.

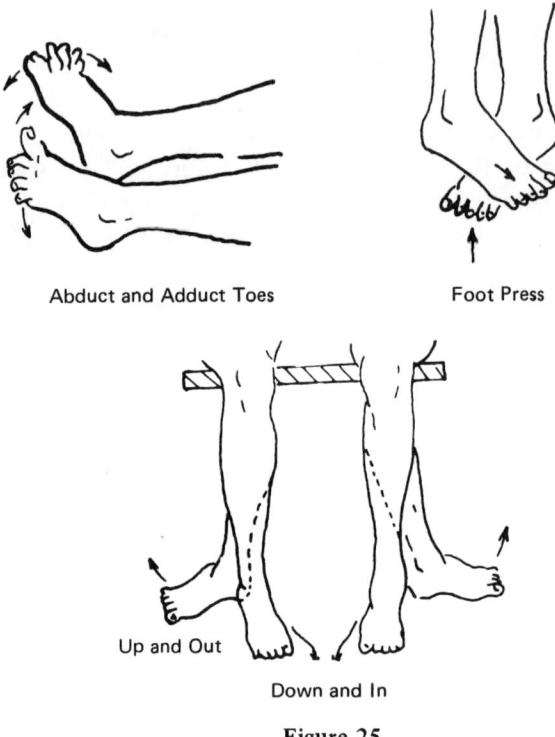

Abduct and Adduct Toes

Foot Press

Up and Out

Down and In

Figure 25
Foot Exercises

If you have pain on the outside of your foot and taping and resting for one to two days do not help the problem, you should see a doctor and have X-rays taken. You may have a fracture of the styloid process of the fifth metatarsal.

Of course, there can be fractures of any one of the bones in the arch, and sprains of any of the ligaments between the joints and bones of the foot. Injuries that do not respond quickly to rest should be investigated by a physician, especially if there is pain with walking.

Problems in the ball of the foot can be quite debilitating to athletes. One of the more common is callus on the bottom of the foot. These calluses are thickened tissue formed by the body as a protective mechanism against damaging the metatarsal heads on the ball of the foot. They often are caused by one of the metatarsal heads being lower than adjacent ones. Thus,

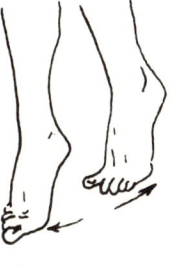

Raising on Toes

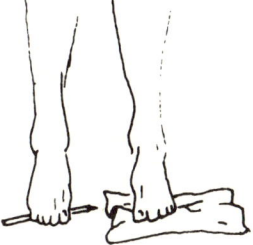

Toe Pick Up
Pencil and Towel

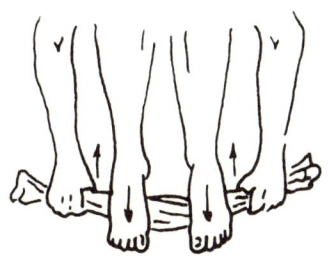

Towel Pull

Figure 25 (cont.)
Foot Exercises

there is more shearing force between the bones and the skin. Forefoot varus and forefoot valgus cause a locking of the foot with rocking of the skin underneath the metatarsal heads. This pinching and shearing causes deep, painful calluses.

Calluses are difficult to distinguish from warts. Warts tend to be more circular in nature and to cause more pain than calluses. Unlike calluses, if warts are trimmed with a razor blade, a small amount of bleeding takes place. Warts usually hurt when there is lateral pressure, whereas calluses hurt more when there is direct pressure. Finally, there are skin lines in calluses, and these lines do not penetrate into warts.

A wart is a virus infection that may be transmitted from one part of the body to another or from person to person. I usually treat warts chemically, since this does not debilitate the athlete. It usually works well and no scar is left.

Treatment of calluses is a different story. Initially, I trim the calluses, then balance the foot in some form of orthotic to help disperse the stress along the bottom of the foot. Occasionally, the calluses are so painful and deep that even balancing the foot will not help, because the metatarsal is low and won't go back to its original place. If this is the case, then a surgical procedure called an osteotomy is done. The bone is cut so that the metatarsal heads are level with the adjacent ones. This surgery can be done under local anesthesia but usually takes the athlete out of competition for six to eight weeks while the fracture created by the surgery is healing.

In older persons, there can also be problems on the ball of the foot due to an atrophic fat pad. There is normally a lot of fat on the bottom of the foot, but with age we may lose some of the fat and therefore lose protection under the metatarsal heads. When this happens, orthotics wth protective material must be used. A shuffling type of running gait with a more flat-footed stride is usually more comfortable than a form which causes the runner to place more stress on the ball of the foot. Softer surfaces also help.

Another common injury is a stress fracture in the metatarsals. This usually occurs from unaccustomed stress or from rapid increases in mileage. The bones are not ready for this stress, so they initially respond by weakening themselves in preparation for a strengthening process. Additional mileage causes additional stress to the bone during this weakened phase and cracks the bone. Stress fractures of the metatarsals should be treated by taping the foot and placing it in a firm wooden shoe for three to four weeks, then gradually returning to running on grass for another three weeks. If the runner ignores the pain of the stress fracture and continues working out on hard surfaces, there is a chance the stress fracture will become a complete fracture. This will then take a good eight to twelve weeks to heal.

The toes themselves can have bothersome calluses or corns. Many athletes tape their toes so the corns will not hurt during running. Likewise, shoes can be modified for toe problems by placing elastic in the toe box or simply by slitting the toe box with a knife. Runners whose toes are so badly deformed or have such painful corns over bony projections that running is impossible need surgical correction. Surgery on toes is relatively easy, the results are predictably good, and the athlete is away from running for a minimum amount of time.

Neuroma problems in the ball of the foot (see chapter 7) must be distinguished from other pain in that area. It is common to have bursitis under metatarsal heads, and the diagnosis between bursitis and neuroma can sometimes be difficult. However, a doctor well versed in sports medicine usually has little trouble making this distinction.

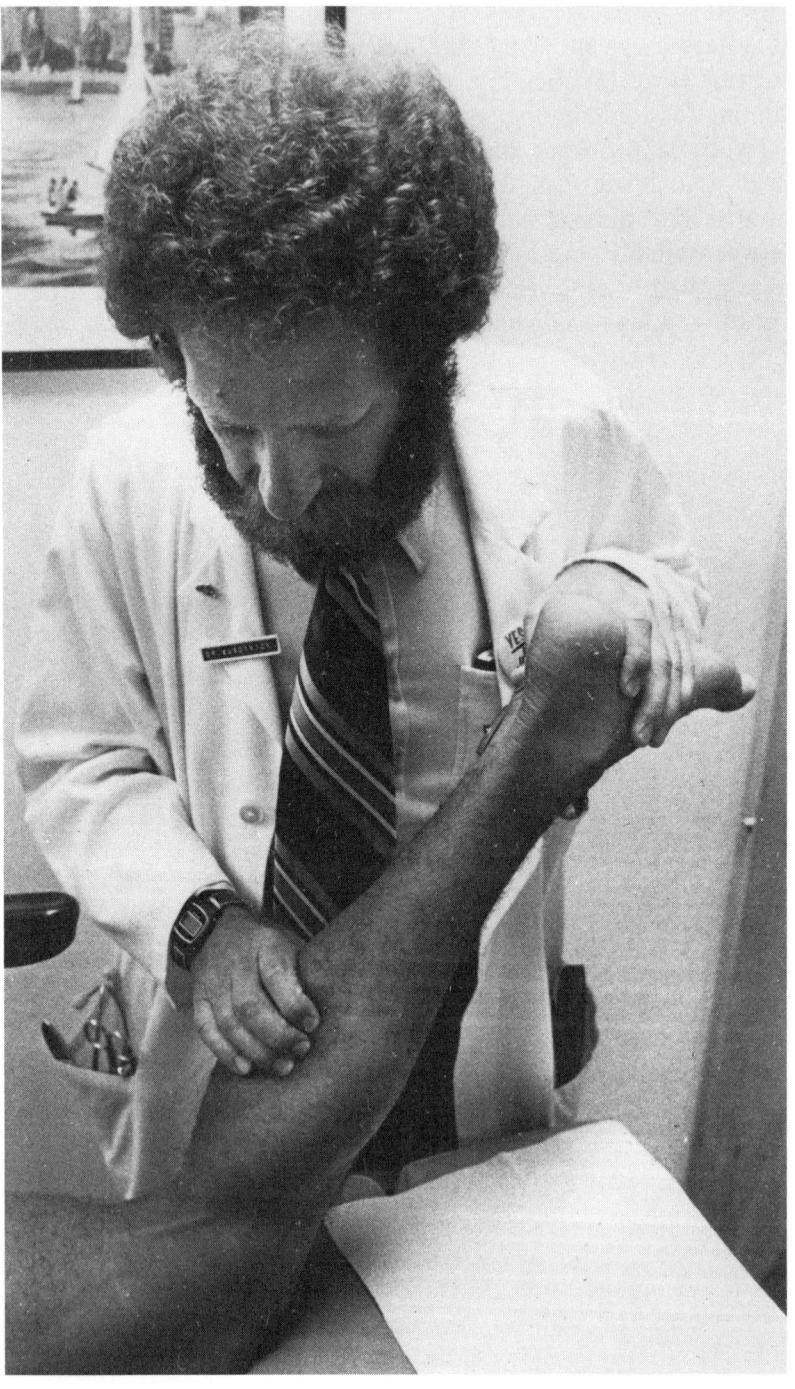

10

Leg Injuries

Don was 36 years old, had been running 30 miles a week for two years and had never been injured. He'd had the usual annoyances of running—sore legs, mild achilles strain, even runner's knee. But these had all responded to backing off on mileage until the pain disappeared and replacing worn shoes sooner. He wore down the outside of his shoe heels quickly, more so than his friends. He also was bowlegged and had a rather higharched foot which absorbed shock poorly. But none of this concerned him while he remained healthy.

Don decided that after two years of running and several lowkey races it was time for the big one—the marathon. He chose the Avenue of the Giants race as his first. He planned to increase his mileage gradually to 60 a week over a period of three months.

At 50 miles a week, Don noted some soreness in the upper shin. With only a month to go, he ignored the soreness and increased his mileage to 60 per week. On one long run, the ache became pain, the run became a walk and then a limp. The next day, walking was again comfortable, but on each succeeding day when he attempted to run there was pain.

Don took aspirin and wrapped the leg in an Ace bandage, but there was still too much pain for him to run normally. He tried to run on grass; still too much pain. He rode his bike, thinking that his "shin splints" would surely respond.

After one week, running still was impossible. The marathon was quickly approaching. Reservations had been confirmed. Time off from work was planned. Yet Don could not run. Aspirin, ice, tape, and new shoes did not help.

"How could such a small area of pain be so intense and so disabling?" he asked me. "Doc, can't you just give me some cortisone shots, orthotics, and maybe a different shoe?"

I responded that I couldn't do what he requested. Shin splints that do not respond to rest are stress fractures until proven otherwise. I told him no running for six weeks and then only on grass at first.

Don asked to see the fracture on X-rays. I told him it was too early, that we would not see it for three to six weeks, or until the fracture was nearly healed. So Don cancelled his reservations, and swam and biked. He also did light weight-training. A few weeks later, new X-rays showed the healing fracture. And three weeks after that, Don started running on grass and increased his weight training for the injured leg.

He had a good base to build upon, a good background from the two years of running. But he had to come back slowly, because for every week away from running with an injury you lose three weeks of training.

Eight months later, Don broke four hours in his first marathon. His modest foot imbalances (his arch was too high) had been corrected with a Sporthotic.

High-arched feet do not absorb shock well. Stress is transmitted to the bone and may be involved with stress reactions. With Don's increase in mileage, orthotics became necessary to help the foot absorb more shock. Whereas he could function well at 30 miles a week without orthotics, the increase in mileage caused new demands upon the body. His modest foot imbalance was a factor in the stress fracture. (For more on stress fractures, see chapter 13.)

INSIDE OF LEG PAIN

Pain on the inside of the leg is most commonly caused by shin splint syndrome, a catch-all term which describes three or four different processes.

A common problem is tendinitis of one or more of the tendons on the inside of the leg—the flexor tendons which tend the great toe or lesser toes or the posterior tibial tendon which helps hold up the medial longitudinal arch. Tendinitis usually occurs in the lower one-fourth of the leg in the area of the inner ankle bone.

At the point where the tendons join their muscles, there can be a strain of the myotendinous junction, or there may be a strain of the muscle higher up; this is called myositis. Along with tendinitis and myositis, there can be pain at the attachment of the muscle to the bone in the middle one-third of the leg; we call this periostitis. The tibia bone itself also can be overworked and can develop small cortical cracks called multiple stress fractures. Before these cracks appear, the bone itself is overworked, sore, and inflamed—a syndrome called multiple stress reaction of bone.

If periostitis is present, it is possible to run your finger along the bone where the muscles attach and to feel little lumps which indicate inflammation. Deep massage may smooth out these lumps.

The most common cause of shin splint injuries is overpronation of the foot. With pronation, the posterior tibial muscle-tendon unit is strained as it works overtime to hold up the arch and slow down excessive rotations of the leg. In an attempt to use the toes too much, the flexor muscles become strained, and tendinitis or myositis can occur. As pronation increases, there is a gradual pulling away of the muscles from the bone; thus, myositis, periostitis, and stress reaction of bone develop.

Another factor should be considered. The muscles have a protective function in helping to support the architectural structures of the bone. They help diminish stress at contact. When the muscles get fatigued, the bone bears more stress and then is more easily fractured. Indeed, there may be fatigue fractures of the tibia with unaccustomed mileage or too rapid an increase in training.

The treatment for the problems of the inner aspect of the leg are centered around physical therapy. I prefer contrast baths which alternate one minute of ice massage with one minute of warm compresses. This should be done for at least twelve minutes. It is helpful to use these contrast baths after workouts and heat alone before workouts. However, if there is a lot of swelling, use ice alone for six minutes. You can take a paper or styrofoam cup, fill it with water, and place it in the freezer. When you return from the workout, use this ice applicator for six minutes of massage. Follow this with ten minutes of deep massage.

Next, we must look at biomechanics. Any foot which is excessively pronated should be protected or balanced with a foot orthotic. Likewise, we should look at the shoes. Shoes with a flimsy counter which allow too much rotation, or which have too narrow a heel should be exchanged for more proper ones. Your sports podiatrist can help you with this choice, as can a shoe salesman if he is a knowledgeable runner.

Of course, softer surfaces are always helpful with shin splint problems. I suggest running on grass or dirt and staying off roads until the pain subsides. I often find that my athletes do much better running every other day to give their overused tissue a day of rest between training sessions.

The shin splint syndrome may need some form of medication such as two aspirin a half-hour before running. More advanced problems require X-rays and stronger forms of anti-inflammatory medication. Taping with elastic tape often helps, because it holds the tendons and muscles against the bone and prevents them from pulling loose. Likewise, arch taping is helpful before fast running.

FRONT OF LEG PAIN

Pain in the front of the leg can be called anterior shin splints or compartment syndrome of the antigravity muscles. These muscles, the anterior tibial and extensor, come down the front of the leg and foot. Their main function is to decelerate the foot as you land heel-first and the forefoot slaps to the ground. The muscles are supposed to ease the transition from the swing phase to heel contact and midstance of gait. However, if you are running extremely fast on hard surfaces, there is a tendency for the surfaces, gravity, and speed to throw your foot to the surface, stretching and straining the antigravity muscles.

The calf muscles make up four-fifths of the bulk of the lower leg, and the antigravity muscles make up only one-fifth. The latter, however, have to be strong enough to fight against the overpull of the gravity muscles. The antigravity muscles, be they the muscles in the front of the leg or front of the thigh, usually are weak in runners and need continual attention. (On the other hand, the muscles in the back of the leg and thigh tend to become tight and need continual stretching.)

As a preventive measure against weak antigravity muscles, a five-pound weight can be fashioned out of an old paint can with gravel in it. This is placed over the foot, usually with the shoe on so that the wire from the can will not injure the foot. The athlete sits on a table and moves his foot up and down to strengthen the muscles in the front of the leg (*fig. 26*). Extensive stretching of the calf muscles is also helpful.

With anterior shin splints, there is usually pain to the front and outside of the leg. There is more pain when the athlete stands on his heel and pulls his toes up to the front of the leg, because he uses the antigravity muscles. The initial treatment is taking care of the inflammation by resting or running on softer surfaces, and by applying ice for six minutes after running, then massaging with the fingers to break up any adhesions or

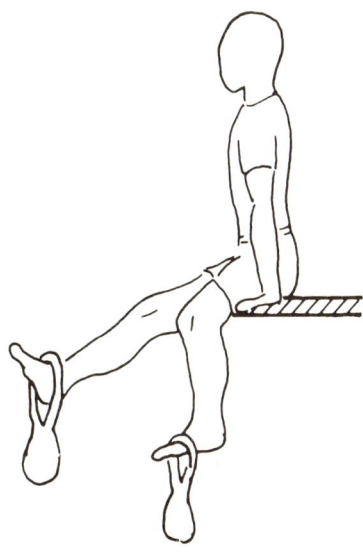

Figure 26
Front-of-Leg Exercises

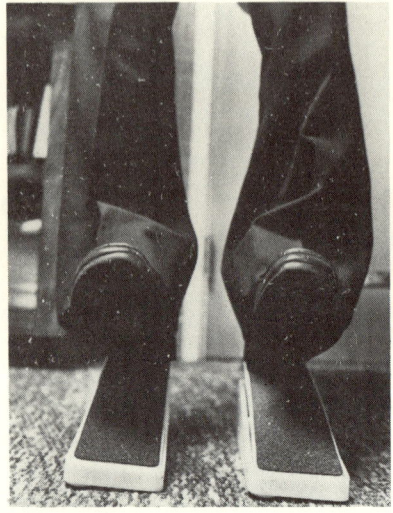

Flex Wedges are handy for achilles, calf, and anterior muscle stretching.

scar tissue which may have formed. If pain persists, X-rays should be taken to rule out stress fractures. Some form of orthotic may help stabilize the stride and decrease abnormal wobbling of the foot at contact which places additional stress on the antigravity muscles.

Runners who have an excessively high-arched foot and a dropped forefoot may place additional strain on the antigravity muscles because the forefoot is lower than the heel and the muscles have to work overtime to pull the forefoot up. An orthotic with an eighth-inch heel lift is often helpful with these problems.

Biomechanically, the problem may be overstriding, and the athlete must be taught to use a shorter stride and have the heel land just below the center of gravity. If the foot lands in front of the body, then the ground pushes the foot backward and causes more stress on the foot and leg in the anterior compartment.

If there is excessive pain, an anterior compartment syndrome may be present. This is much more serious than shin splints because numbness may persist and there may be damage to the nerve. If you have shin splints, elevate your foot and leg and immediately apply ice. If the injury does not respond to this within one hour, see a sports podiatrist, general surgeon, or orthopedist. At times, a release of the fascia is necessary to relieve pressure built up in this closed compartment. If this is not taken care of immediately, there can be extensive muscle damage and permanent deformity of the lower extremity. Surgery for shin splints is usually done in patients who have chronic problems. It can be done for any compartment where there is excessive damage and swelling due to overuse or faulty biomechanics. Sometimes, changes in the tissue form a gristle-like material, and everytime you run there is pain. Before surgery is undertaken, the doctor should rule out stress reactions of bone, multiple little cracks which heal with rest and time. Of course, if the athlete has rested for six months, tries to run and still has pain, it is obvious that the bone would have healed. Something else is wrong.

Jeff Stark was such a patient. He came to me complaining of anterior compartment syndrome and other overuse syndromes. I gave him orthotics, exercises, ice, and everything else I thought might help. We worked together extensively and even used injections into the anterior compartment to ease swelling and pressure. Nothing helped.

Jeff eventually had surgery on his leg to free the muscle from the bone. He had periostitis, meaning the attachment of the muscle to the bone was inflamed. He also had myositis; the muscles were somewhat inflamed within a very tight muscle sheath. Once this was released and the pressure was off the muscles, Jeff was able to rehabilitate himself and become a painfree runner again.

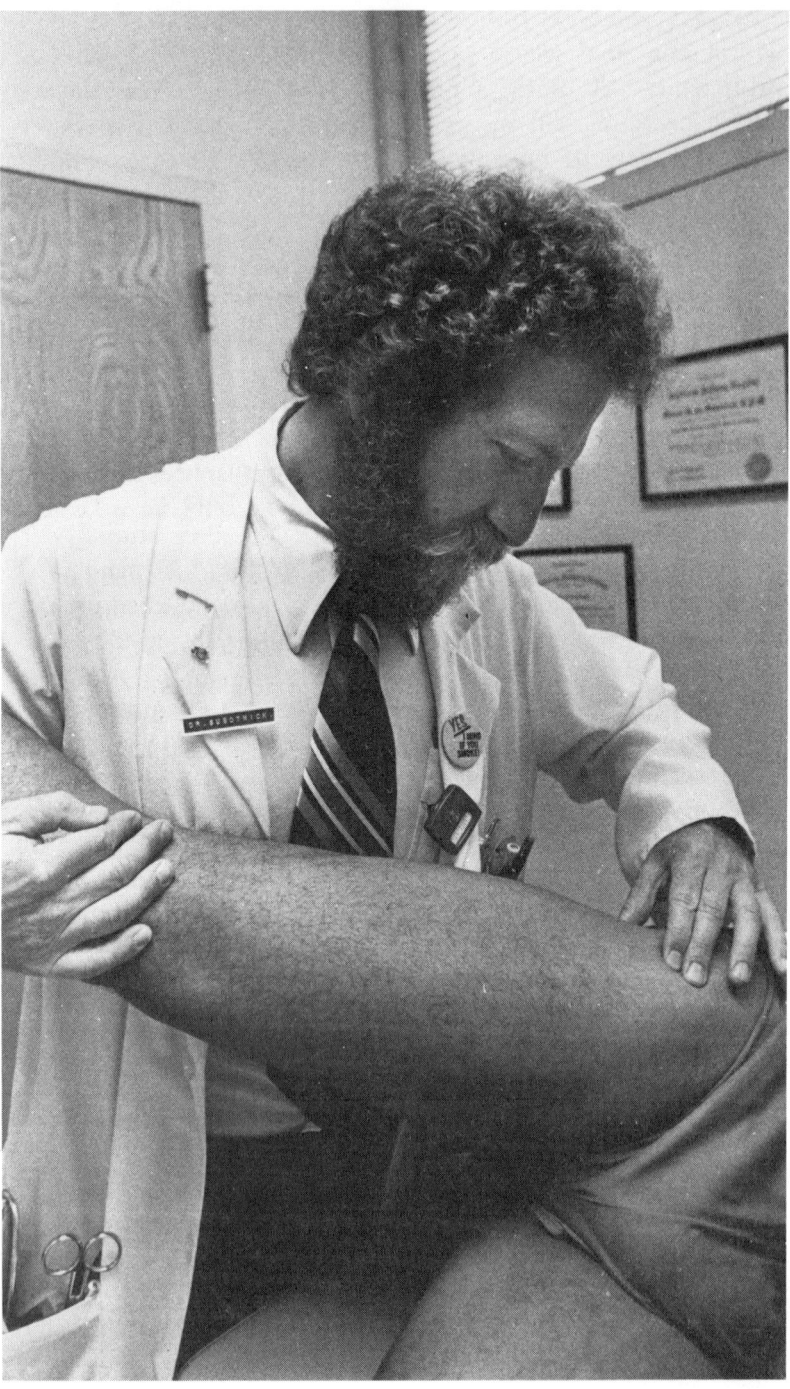

11

Hip Injuries

Because of my own determination and perhaps stupidity, I became the victim of an injury called an iliotibial band syndrome. (The iliotibial band connects the hip and knee on the outside of the leg. While my problem mainly affected the knee, the hip was also involved.)

A marathon is 26-plus miles. It takes approximately one month to recover from a marathon if it is run with a sustained effort. It can take up to eight weeks to recover fully from an all-out effort. However, I once ran a marathon in Dallas and just a week later ran one in Hawaii.

My plan was to use the Dallas marathon as a training run for Honolulu. I was going to try to set a personal record in the latter race. But there as excitement in the air at the start of the Dallas marathon. After a mile, I found myself running alongside a pleasant young woman with a good stride. I stayed with her for four or five miles, even though she kept a faster pace than I had planned to run. Then, George Sheehan ambled up on my right. I decided to run with him, and we quickly left the company of the woman.

Our pace became faster. I felt that if I got tired, I could always slow down. However, George and I felt a kind of electricity that day. Before long, I realized we were running close to a three-hour pace. I was going to run a personal best. George also realized this and told me to go on. My pace eventually slowed, but I still ran 3:13.

The next morning, I was awakened by a phone call from Harry Cordellos. Harry is a blind runner who has been my patient and friend for years. He'd finished the Dallas marathon seconds before me. He suggested we go on a nice little 10-mile run, and I did it because my musculoskeletal system felt fine.

The following morning, I was somewhat sore and stiff. But I still didn't feel nearly as bad as I normally do after a marathon. It hit me the day after that; my left leg tightened up. If I walked up or down stairs, or ran much more than four or five miles, I stiffened up over the outside of my leg.

My iliotibial band was moving forward over the bones on the outside of my knee, causing a painful snapping sensation. To compensate for this, I altered my gait and ran in-toed. This gave some relief but caused aching on the lateral side of my knee around the patella. If I toed out again, my iliotibial band was painful, and the medial side of my kneecap hurt.

To complicate this, because my muscles were stiff and sore I was running somewhat awkwardly and swinging my legs in a circumducted manner. I began feeling snapping and pain over the hip.

The Honolulu marathon was approaching. I knew I was still going to run it, and I knew I was in trouble. My iliotibial band was no longer a nuisance, but a real problem. There was extreme pain when going downhill. In fact, I looked forward to the uphill portions of the run.

Several days before the marathon, I received a cortisone injection to ease the inflammation. This made walking and running more comfortable, and I hoped the effects would carry on through the race. They didn't.

Two miles into the marathon, my whole left side started tightening up. I found myself running awkwardly. At the halfway mark, I realized that this was more of an ordeal than a race, and it would take all I had just to finish with the pain in my leg. I managed to get through it in a little over 3:30. If nothing else, it taught me the importance of fully recovering after a marathon.

Soreness was still present two weeks later. I injected a small amount of Xylocaine with long- and short-acting cortisone along the insertion of my iliotibial band, then applied ultrasound to disperse the injection. Icing for six minutes followed each workout. Of course, I continued to stretch.

Three weeks after the Honolulu marathon, I finished a workout which included hills and intervals. It was painless.

HIP PAIN

Pain on the outside of a runner's hip is most commonly caused by the iliotibial band syndrome. A muscle called the tensor fascia lata is broad, short, and flat and lies over the outside of the hip. From it arises a slender tendinous band which inserts into the outside of the tibia bone just below the hip.

This whole structure acts as a stabilizer for the femur. With increased mileage or unaccustomed activity, it becomes fatigued and tightens. When this happens, it can snap over the knee joint to produce iliotibial band syndrome of the knee (see chapter 5), or it can snap over the greater trochanter of the hip (*fig. 27*). At the same time, bursitis of the greater trochanter can develop.

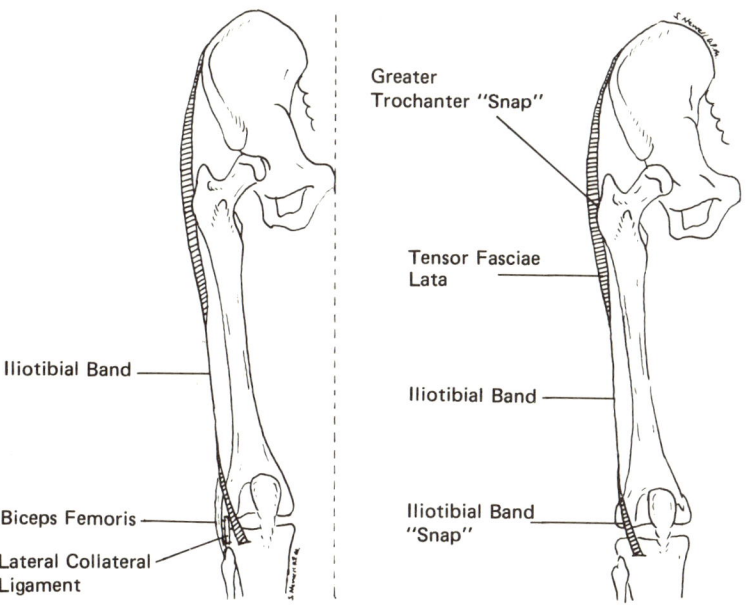

Greater Trochanter "Snap"

Tensor Fasciae Lata

Iliotibial Band

Iliotibial Band "Snap"

Iliotibial Band

Biceps Femoris

Lateral Collateral Ligament

Figure 27
Iliotibial Band Syndrome (Hip)

There is usually a lot of pain along with a popping or snapping sensation. The runner feels like his hip is going out of joint or that something is seriously wrong within the joint. However, a sports podiatrist or orthopedist can make a diagnosis readily, and treatment is rather simple. This includes stretching the tensor fascia lata and iliotibial band, and strengthening this muscle with lateral leg lifts (*fig. 28*).

If there is imbalance in the foot, orthotics are helpful. Also, with any type of leg, foot, or back problem—but especially with hip problems—limb-length discrepancies should be checked. There may be a true limb-length discrepancy with one bone longer than the other, or there may be a functional problem with one foot flatter than the other, creating an apparent discrepancy which goes away when the feet are balanced.

Limb-length discrepancies in runners are much more serious than in the general walking population. Because of the "rule of three" which states there is three time more body weight going through the feet during running than during walking, I multiply everything by three. Thus, if a runner has a one-eighth-inch short leg, it is as though he has a *three-eighths-inch* shortage. This is enough to cause problems. Low-back pain and pain on the

Figure 28
Lateral Leg Lifts

outside of the hip can occur. The short-leg side is usually the one that has problems, because there is an overstride as the short leg tries to catch up with the long one. There is more shock at contact, which is farther back on the heel, and more strain on the whole leg.

If the short-leg syndrome is not present, and there is still the iliotibial band syndrome or a greater trochanteric problem on the outside of the hip (and stretching, physical therapy with ice, avoidance of hills, and similar practices have failed) then an orthopedist may wish to inject cortisone into the bursa. This usually works quite well, and the athlete should not worry about side-effects with this type of treatment. The injection goes into the bursa, not the hip joint. However, before injec-tions are given, the athlete and doctor may wish to consider oral inflammatory medication. Aspirin is useful, and stronger ications are at times more effective.

p pain in youngsters may be caused by pulling on the th plates, stress fractures (as in adults), or tendinitis (hip ers). A sports physician or orthopedist should be consulted. s are helpful. Hip arthritis may be a problem in older its.

12

Sciatica and Low-Back Injuries

Charles Freeman was getting ready for his first marathon when he developed sciatica on the right side. Chronic mild pain radiated down the inside of his leg. He hurt more if he laid on his back and raised his leg up, a giveaway clue for sciatica.

I examined him and found that he had Morton's foot with five degrees of forefoot varus. I also found a one-eighth-inch short right leg. He had orthotics from another podiatrist which appeared to allow his foot to pronate too much.

Treatment consisted of making new orthotics with a one-eighth-inch heel lift. Charles was placed on exercises to strengthen his abdominal muscles and on stretching exercises. His sciatica soon went away, but his troubles were far from over.

Freeman increased his mileage and began running faster. He soon returned with his first case of shin splints. I examined him and found, even with the new orthotics, that he pronated too much, pulling the muscles on the insides of his legs. Thus, more posting or varus control was placed on the orthotics to help rest these muscles. I also gave him special strengthening exercises to build the muscles on the insides of his legs.

A month later, he noted that he was getting better but still had some pain in his legs. I had him demonstrate to me the exercises he was doing and found out he was spending most of the time strengthening the *fronts* of his legs. His shin splint problem was on the inside, involving the posterior tibial and flexor tendons. When I showed him how to isolate the proper muscles by pressing his feet together and he began seriously to strengthen these muscles, his shin splint problem quickly went away.

Charles again increased his mileage, started running faster, racing, and doing hills. And he began experiencing knee problems. He was told to work on strengthening the muscles in the fronts of his thighs, and because he was running very fast was given Sporthotic devices which were more flexible and allowed him to have a springier gait when running. They still provided the amount of control necessary for his shin splint, knee, and sciatica problems.

I continued seeing Charles for various problems related to training too hard or running too fast. He eventually ran his first marathon in 3:03, a fairly spectacular debut. But after the race, he started hurting on his right hip and experienced the all-too-familiar greater trochanteric bursitis. This happened because the muscles on the outside of the hip and leg fatigued late in the marathon and became tight. They then started snapping and rubbing over bony prominences. After I showed how to stretch these muscles, he recovered.

Charles Freeman's case illustrates how a runner can develop a series of apparently unrelated injuries which actually share the same basic causes. It also shows how a runner cures one problem, then moves to a new level of speed or distance to find a new way to hurt himself. Everyone has weak links and breaking points.

SCIATIC PAIN

Sciatica means there is something wrong with the sciatic nerve. Pain shoots from the back, radiating underneath the buttocks, down the inside and back portions of the thigh, and farther down the leg. There is usually pain if the athlete lies on his back and does a straight leg raise.

When sciatica is present, you should be examined for limb-length discrepancy and for foot imbalance. Along with this, you should be checked for low-back pathology, damage to the

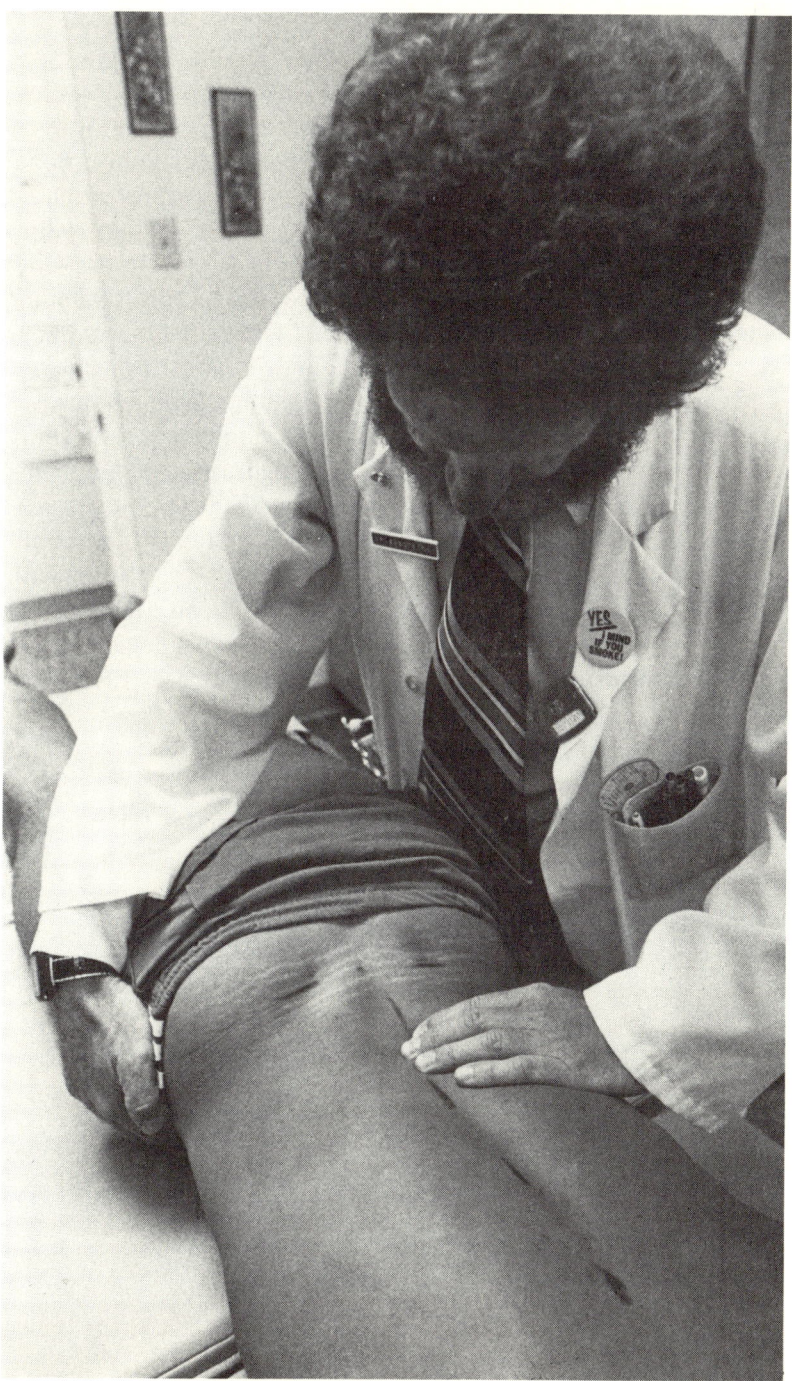

sciatic nerve itself or any of the other low-back nerves. The sports podiatrist may wish to consult with an orthopedist when sciatica is present, especially if this does not respond readily to heel lifts, orthotics, stretching exercises, and other conventional treatment. (Low-back pain may be caused by serious problems such as arthritis which conservative treatment will not help.)

Sciatica is a difficult problem, but with athletes it often does respond to simple exercises. One of the most useful stretching exercises involves the gluteal muscles. It is done by placing your heel on a high stool and slowly bending forward to stretch out the buttocks muscles. You can also take your thigh and press it against your abdomen or pull your knee up toward your tummy (*fig. 29*). When the gluteal muscles get tight, they press on the sciatic nerve.

Along with the stretching exercises, it is extremely important to strengthen the abdominal muscles. Do bent-knee situps with your heels tucked as close to your buttocks as you can and your knees really bent. Put your hands behind your head and then sit halfway up instead of all the way. Do thirty-five to fifty bent-knee situps daily. Yoga really helps!

Figure 29
Sciatic Exercises

Hill running often causes sciatica. Going uphill, the gluteal muscles get tight, and going downhill there is overstriding and increased shock which can damage this nerve. Likewise, athletes who have occupations which cause them to sit on the edge of the chair may get a sciatic compression syndrome. This is relieved by changing sitting positions or by getting a foam-rubber seat. The athlete also has to be taught to straighten his back. The anterior iliac crest must be rotated upward or toward the head. When the athlete is lying on his back with the knees bent, he must be able to press a sponge down flat under the small of his back. When this is done, much of the back pain is relieved.

Sciatica and low-back pain often are helped by chiropractic manipulation. But while this relieves the immediate pain, it does not solve the problem. Further consultation with a sports podiatrist or orthopedist may be needed.

13

Stress Fractures

Bartlett Waide had been running 30 miles a week when he
came in for a preventive checkup. He wished to increase his
mileage (his goal was 10 miles a day) and to avoid problems
often associated with such a step. He noted that his left ankle
sprained frequently; he had sprained it twice in the past six
months.

My initial evaluation showed that he had a sinus tarsi syndrome with some anterior capsulitis. This means the entrance to
the subtalar joint, the one beneath the ankle bone, was somewhat strained. (Ligaments in this opening to the subtalar joint
are sprained more often than the ankle joint itself. This is usually not treated, even though the ankle sprain itself is treated.)

Waide's treatment consisted of a foot support to hold the
heel in a more neutral position, and a mixed cortisone injection
into the sinus tarsi to dissolve some of the scar tissue which had
formed around the torn ligaments. I placed him on a rehabilitative program for the ankle which consisted of jumping rope for
balance and strength, and running figure-eights. I also told him
to build up the peroneal muscles on the ankle with weights and
with resistance exercises for the outside of the foot.

The treatment worked so well that Bartlett rapidly doubled
his mileage to about 10 a day. Both of us should have known
that the way to increase mileage is *slowly*. Not long after the
ankle had healed, he began having pain which he assumed was

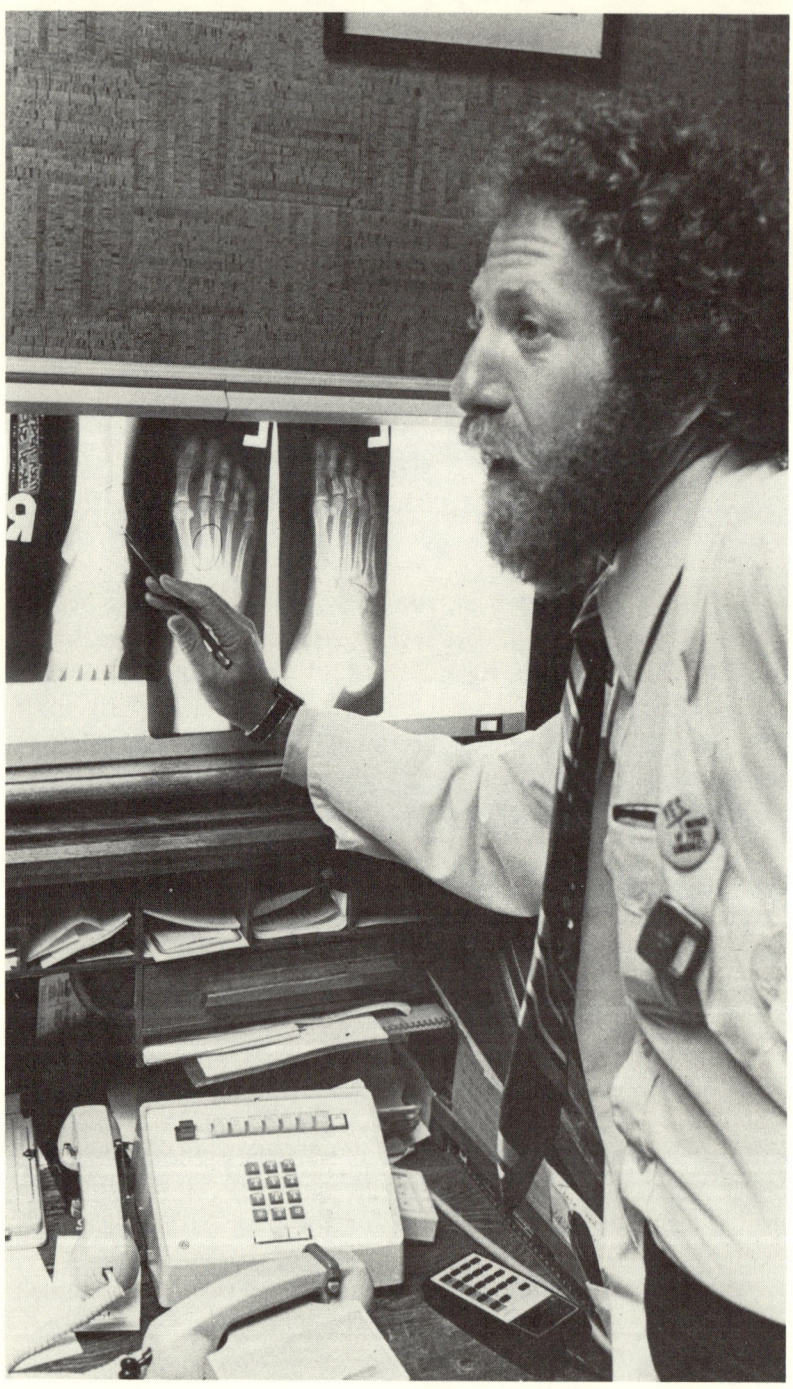

shin splints in the left leg. The pain was in the lower one-third of the leg, over the tibia and to the inside of the leg. I initially thought this was shin splints or a muscle pull.

Bartlett was treated as having shin splints and told to use pain as an indication of what he could and could not do, to run to the point of discomfort but not through pain. He was instructed to take two aspirin a half-hour before running and to stay on softer surfaces. He had been running on hills, emphasizing downhill work. Initially, I gave him anti-inflammatory medication to go along with the aspirin, but this did little good.

He did not respond to conservative treatment—aspirin, icing for six minutes after running, decreased training, and anti-inflammatory pills. Therefore, I suspected a stress fracture might be present. I took X-rays of the leg about three weeks after the onset of pain and saw no fracture, but I still felt he might have one.

Bartlett returned three weeks later, still having pain. I took another X-ray. Sure enough, the stress fracture was visible as a small crack in the cortex or outer portion of the tibia; healing had taken place. Usually, with stress fractures or any type of fracture, the changes in the bone are two to three weeks behind on X-ray. In other words, when I finally made the definitive diagnosis of stress fracture by X-ray, the fracture was almost healed.

I explained to Waide that he had violated the rule which so many people do—"too much, too soon." He smiled and agreed. He said his foot and ankle felt so good after I treated it with medication and orthotics that he rapidly increased his mileage and hurt himself.

The morals to this story are (1) too much, too soon leads to injury (2) tendinitis or shin splint syndrome that does not respond fairly quickly to decreased training, aspirin, and ice is a stress fracture until proven otherwise and (3) stress fracture is a reaction of bone to accumulated stress, akin to the bending of a wire coat hanger until it gets hot and then snaps.

STRESS FRACTURE PAIN

Stress fractures are just what the name implies—fractures from overstress. They can occur in the foot, leg, thigh, or even up around the hip joint. No bone in the lower extremity is completely exempt from stress fractures.

Stress fractures of the foot usually occur suddenly. There is swelling on top of the foot, and the athlete thinks he may have extensor tendinitis. The redness and pain, however, do not go away and there is great pain if the athlete attempts to run—even on soft surfaces. When an X-ray is taken, it usually shows nothing until two to three weeks after the injury, because X-rays of bone usually lag this far behind with stress fractures. Three weeks after the traumatic incident, the X-ray has signs of demineralization along the fracture line, and after four to six weeks there is evidence of healing where new bone is formed.

Harry Cordellos, the blind runner from San Francisco, had a stress fracture. I knew it was present, but it did not show up on X-ray until *seven* weeks after the incident. I have had patients with stress fractures of the tibia that did not show up until eight weeks after the incident.

My philosophy is that if there is pain in the lower extremity that does not respond to rest, it is a stress fracture until proven otherwise. This is especially true of the metatarsal bones, the outer ankle bone and upper tibia.

I first treat stress fractures of the foot by using some measure to stop the pain. If there is pain with running and minimal pain just with walking, I use a wooden shoe, felt padding for the arch, and taping to immobilize the foot (*fig. 30*). No running is allowed for three weeks, yet the athlete may swim or ride a bike. After three weeks, he may run on softer surfaces while taped and then slowly build up his mileage until, at six weeks, he returns to harder surfaces. The athlete is cautioned that the reason he had a stress fracture was that he overstressed the bone. Too much, too soon was the straw that broke the runner's bone.

Stress fractures of the heel are treated with some form of heel cup or heel pad and six weeks of rest. Stress fractures of the navicular or tarsal bones are usually treated with a cast for four to six weeks. This is because these fractures are in joints which move a lot and are very difficult to heal. A stress fracture there may convert to a complete fracture because of neglect. Surgery with bone grafts is sometimes necessary in these cases.

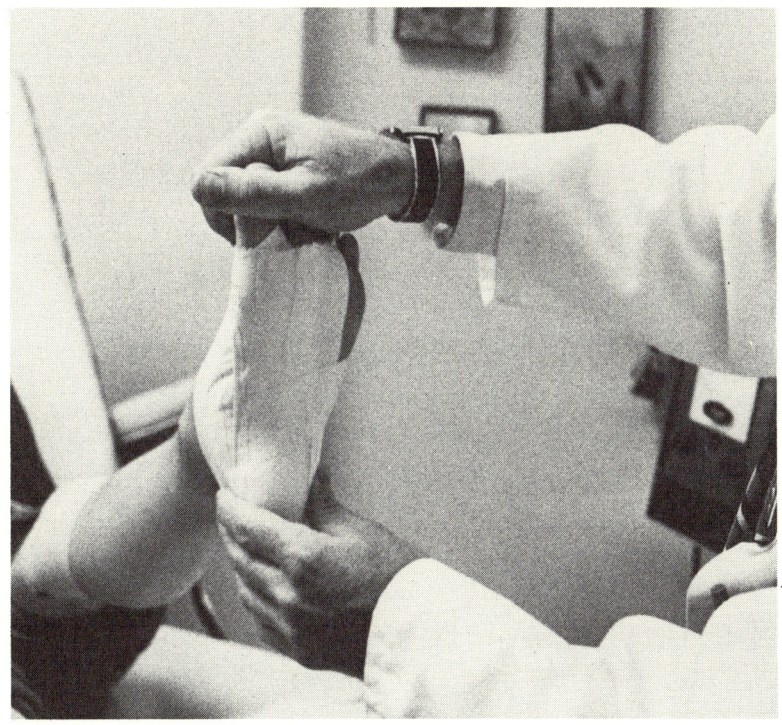

Figure 30
Immobilization of the Foot

Fibular stress fractures are treated with rest for six weeks. No running can be allowed, but a cast is usually not necessary. Following this period, rehabilitative exercises are utilized. We also must look into why the stress fracture occurred in the first place, other than overuse. Often, excessive pronation causes the heel bone to rub on the fibula, and the fibula may be rotating. The fracture usually occurs just above the ankle joint. Orthotics are a preventive measure.

Tibial stress fractures are treated with rest for eight weeks, as are stress fractures of the femur. If there is pain with ambulation, crutches are used until the pain is resolved.

My files are jammed with cases of stress fractures. The worst of these are where people had stress fractures, ignored the pain and converted stress fractures of the ankle into complete fractures which took eight to twelve weeks or longer to heal.

14

Ankle Sprains

Joe Henderson sprained his left ankle when he stepped off a curb while running. He recalled that the outside of his ankle bone almost touched the ground. He limped into my office the next day, hardly able to put any weight on his foot.

X-rays showed no fracture of the foot or ankle, but he had ruptured at least the anterior lateral collateral ligament and possibly a portion of the middle collateral ligaments of his ankle. Joe had a "six-week injury."

First, he had to have his ankle immobilized. The humane thing to do was put the ankle in some form of cast so that he could at least walk. I placed him in a Jones cast. The whole foot and leg below the knee were rolled in a soft cotton-type material, and then plaster was applied on the bottom of the foot and in back of the leg, and secured with Ace bandages. He could move his ankle up and down but could not twist it and reinjure the ligaments.

Joe returned in one week, and all the swelling was gone from the ankle. He had been walking in his cast and had been riding a bike. I removed the cast and gave him physical therapy with ultrasound. Following this, I taped his ankle and gave him a canvas brace. I told him he could start walking more and that he needed rehabilitative exercises. When he initially injured his ankle, he had torn some of the receptor sites in the ligaments which tell the brain he is spraining the ankle. I told him he must

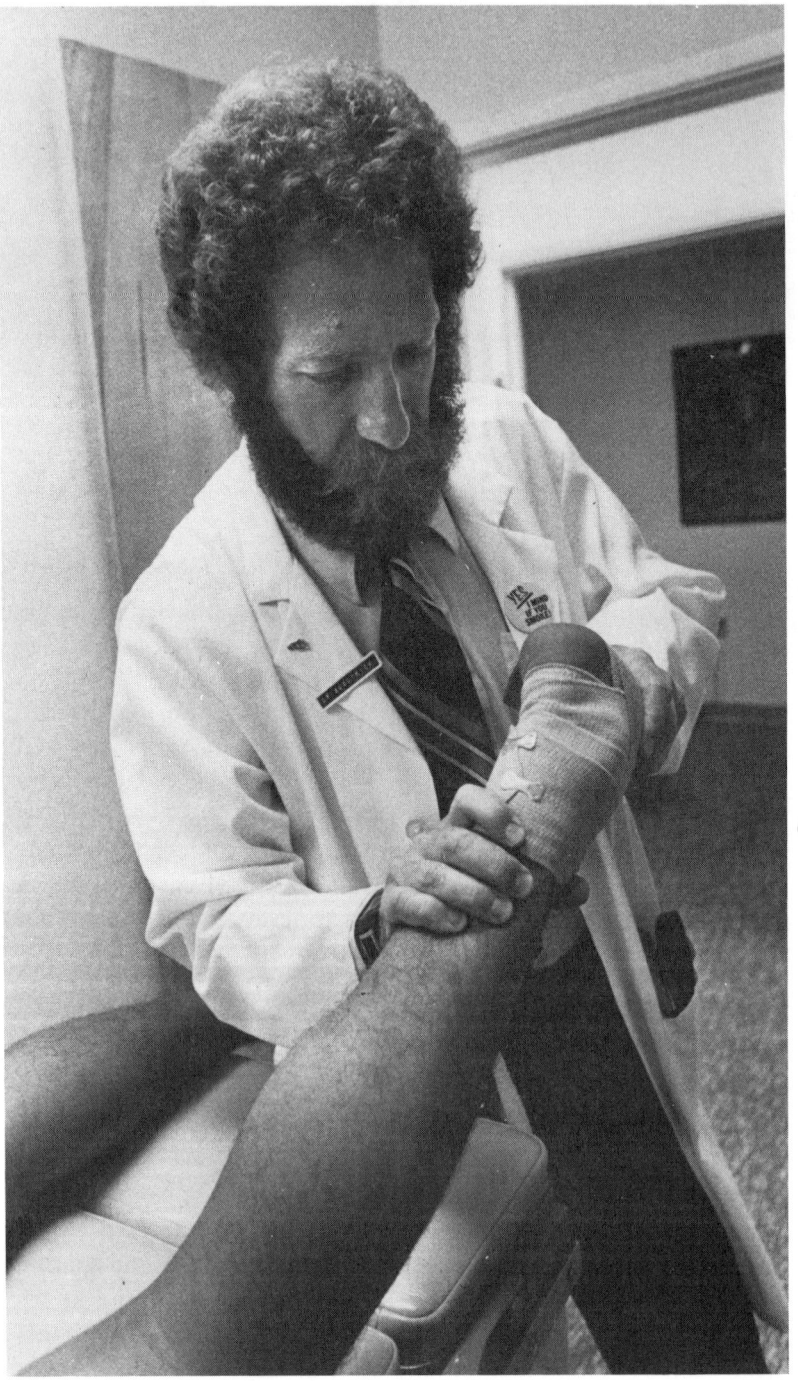

practice balancing on the ankle and eventually start jumping rope to regain his kinesthetic sensations. Otherwise, he might resprain the ankle.

Two weeks after the injury, Henderson began adding small amounts of running (one minute in five) to his hour walks. Within two more weeks, his running apparently was near normal with no ankle pain. However, he noted a weakness which caused him to change his form slightly. He developed pain in his left knee as a result. He also felt that tripling his amount of running in a little more than a week had something to do with this. Once he began using the knee pain as a warning, stopping when it demanded, the knee healed quickly. He had no further problems with either the ankle or knee, and he was able to finish a marathon ten weeks after the injury.

This is not an isolated case. What I show with Joe Henderson's experience is that a debilitating problem can be treated in such a way that very little time away from activity is required and yet proper healing is assured.

If the ankle joint is not treated properly, however, chronic instability results, the runner continually resprains the ankle, and this can even lead to arthritis. The ankle joint sprain is a complicated problem that needs correct medical treatment. Too often, I have been called upon to do surgical procedures to stabilize a weak ankle that wasn't treated properly at the time of the initial injury.

SPRAIN PAIN

Sprained ankles are increasingly prevalent in my practice. One reason is that well-trained athletes daydream on their runs, step off of curbs or into chuckholes, and sprain their ankles. The most common sprain, resulting in pain on the outside of the ankle, is called an inversion sprain (*fig. 31*). The foot turns in under the ankle, stretching and straining the outside ankle ligaments. (Occasionally, just the opposite occurs. The foot pronates too much, causing a sprain on the inside of the ankle. Likewise, a joint farther down in the foot such as the talonavicular joint can be sprained.)

If, following the sprain, the athlete can get up and walk, then

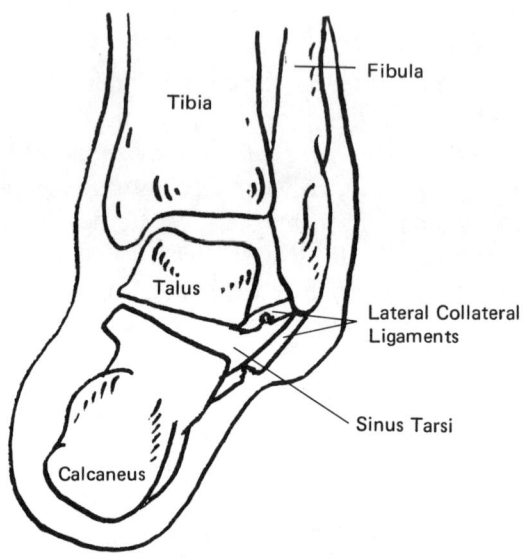

Figure 31
Inversion Ankle Sprain

it is probably not a complete rupture of one of the three ligaments on the outside of the ankle. However, if he cannot jump
up and down on the ball of the foot, there may be something
seriously wrong. A doctor should be consulted at once.

Too often, athletes go home, elevate their foot, put ice on it,
and the next day try to walk around on a grossly painful and
swollen ankle—only to find that they cannot walk. One or two
weeks later, they come to the office and wonder why they are
not healing properly.

Unless it is the kind of sprain that allows you to jump up and
down and to walk without pain, consult a sports-oriented podiatrist or orthopedist immediately. Special tests can be undertaken within the first hour or two, the golden time period
which tells what is wrong. These tests can prevent costly and
more difficult ones in the future.

If a runner comes in with a sprain that has been neglected for
two days and there is a lot of swelling, it is difficult for me to
examine it. Therefore, I get an X-ray to rule out a fracture. It is
possible with a sprained ankle to fracture the outer ankle bone

with an inversion injury. If I am sure there is no fracture, I then do an arthrogram by placing dye in the joint to see how much leakage there is from a tear in the joint capsule. If there is a lot of leakage, I assume that it is an unstable sprain and one of the ligaments around the ankle has been torn. I then must protect this joint for at least three to four weeks to allow the ligaments to heal. If I do not do this, there will be chronic stretching and weakness of the ankle, and arthritis may be the long-term result.

Sprains are often more serious than fractures because they are usually neglected while fractures are treated readily.

TARSAL TUNNEL SYNDROME

Pain on the inner side of the ankle may be the result of tarsal tunnel syndrome. There is pressure on the posterior tibial nerve radiating up the leg and into the foot.

This syndrome may be associated with flexor group tendinitis, excessive pronation, or excessive pressure on the nerve. Orthotics, anti-inflammatory drugs, and injections usually work. Difficult cases respond to surgical decompression of the nerve.

PART III

HEALTH QUESTIONS

15

More Problems

Runners from around the country write and call me as well as come to my office. The one thing they all have in common is they're hurt, can't run normally, and are eager—even desperate—to run again. They want immediate help. I've told in earlier chapters what to do about specific injuries. However, the real point of this book is *prevention*. This final chapter stresses health-maintenance techniques to keep runners from coming to me and other doctors in the numbers they now do.

TYPES OF INJURIES

There are two types of injuries runners may encounter. The first of these injuries is acute, and there is some form of trauma or sudden force which accompanies the injury. The second type of injury is gradual and appears to worsen as the time span increases.

Acute running injuries would consist of ankle sprains from stepping in a chuckhole or perhaps Achilles tendon ruptures from stepping unevenly off a curb. Other forms of acute injuries might be those suffered from being hit by a car. An acute injury obviously needs acute medical care.

The chronic overuse injuries are far more common and have a number of origins. The first of these is biomechanical abnormalities. Examples of these are flatfeet, or one foot with a high arch and the other foot with a low arch, or a person who might have a long leg, short leg or bowlegged deformities. These biomechanical abnormalities are usually small deviations from the ideal body structure, and they are best treated with good running shoes and some form of foot support.

A second cause of overuse injuries might be the sport itself. Specifically the difference between running and walking is that in walking, the feet tend to contact the surface in a parallel fashion and there is a wide base of gait. There may be as much as four to six inches between the feet. When running, one foot will contact the surface in about the same spot as the other foot contacts the surface—in other words, the straight line at about the center of the body.

This difference between running and walking increases the angular deformity of the lower extremities by virtue of the sport itself. There is also a difference in the shock absorbing when comparing running with walking. Normal walking has about one third less stress going through the foot than occurs when running. Of course when walking, one foot is always on the ground, and while running, either both feet are off the ground, or one foot is on the ground.

Another prime cause of overuse injuries is improper conditioning. Conditioning means slowly adapting to stress and the body must do it slowly. Overuse or overstress injuries are from too much stress or too much, too soon. This is common in the beginning runner.

A rule I use is to begin a walking-running program of twenty minutes a day for the first week on level surfaces and slowly increase by not more than five minutes per day per week. It is good to take one or two days off and to do a lot of stretching before and after running.

But what should you do if you notice one of these overuse injuries? If you notice a nagging pain or ache anywhere in the foot, heel, leg, knee, thigh or even low back, the best thing to do is to evaluate exactly what type of difficulty you may be having. In other words, is it pain or discomfort? If it is pain, is it relieved by running, and then does it recur one or two hours after running? If it is discomfort, does it increase throughout the run and become pain at the end of the run? Is it a constant

problem which worsens with running? Does it hurt only with running, or does it hurt when walking and running? This may give you some clue as to what to do.

The rule I use is that you can run with discomfort, but you should not run with an injury. If running causes the problem to worsen, then stop running and see a sports medicine podiatrist. If there is a nagging, aching-type pain, say in the foot, leg or even knee, which is relieved by running but then recurs after running, I would suggest that you continue running but find out why the problem exists. Again, get a good biomechanical checkup by a sports podiatrist.

Check your shoes for abnormal wear. If you are wearing one heel more than the other, you may be overstriding or have a limb-length problem. It is good for an injured runner to slow down, take a shorter stride and to check the shoes and make certain that the heel of the shoe or counter is roughly perpendicular to the supporting surface.

Finally if you hurt so much that you can't run, it is a good idea to find a substitute activity. This should be an aerobic activity like riding a bike or swimming. Also, you should be aware that missing one week from running puts you about three weeks behind in your training schedule if you are preparing for a race. It is important, therefore, to continue with aerobic activity by roughly doubling your resting pulse for 20 to 25 minutes a day.

TOO MUCH, TOO FAST

No matter how much we emphasize it, runners still don't seem to understand that training means gradually adapting to stress. Most of the injuries we see are from overuse. Overuse means increasing mileage from 20 miles one week to 40 the next. Overuse means running 20 miles when you are tired from running 15 miles the day before. Overuse means running as fast as you can for as long as you can when you are not ready for it.

Countless runners are hobbling into podiatrists' offices, seeking magic cures for their problems with orthotics. In reality, although orthotics may help, runners may benefit even more from re-evaluating their own training methods.

The body must adapt slowly to stress. A plateau method of increasing mileage should be used. If you are running 20 miles a week and wish to reach 60 miles, I suggest that you step up by five miles every three weeks—25 miles for three weeks, 30 for the next three, etcetera.

If you increase your running time, you must also increase the amount of time spent stretching and strengthening your muscles before and after running. Most of us, myself included, increase the time we run by decreasing the time we stretch so that we still work out the same total time. If you are sore all the time and are taking aspirin for the pain, then you are running too much, not stretching enough, or both.

I think the best way to run if, for example, you are going to do a 4-mile workout is to do the first mile as *slowly* as you comfortably can, not as fast as you comfortably can. Run the second mile a little bit faster, the third mile faster yet, and save part of the fourth mile for the fastest running. Then, slow down again and finish your run as slowly as you started it so you are relaxed at the end. Finally, devote a good ten to fifteen minutes to stretching exercises.

HOW MUCH IS ENOUGH?

How much running is enough to get the good effects, and how many miles are too many and cause the bad effects? Dr. Tom Bassler of the American Medical Joggers Association says you must do at least six miles a day, live the lifestyle of a marathoner, and have trained enough to complete a marathon. Dr. Bassler says this gives you almost certain immunity from heart disease.

Six miles a day is a popular amount, but even this much causes injuries. Most podiatrists involved in sports medicine feel that anyone running more than 30 miles a week has a much greater chance of being injured than someone running fewer than 30.

Recently, Dr. George Sheehan told me he prefers going long distances every other day with rest days in between. Exercise researchers Dr. David Costill and Dr. Jack Wilmore have said they feel it takes a good day or two of easy running or rest to recover from any type of quality workout. All of us seem to feel that not allowing adequate recovery from hard workouts causes injuries.

Let us assume that six miles a day is enough to get the good effects from running. Let us also assume that with these good effects—relaxation, ability to think clearly, ability to maintain one's vitality, lowering the blood pressure and pulse, etcetera—comes the chance of being injured. Let us say that you run as I do—8 or 9 miles a day with 11- to 15-mile runs on the weekends, with perhaps one day off every two weeks.

Chances are that you have aches and pains which mean you should slow down, and you are hurt at least twice a year to the extent that you have to rest. Chances are if you had rested when you had the aches and pains, you wouldn't have had to take the more prolonged periods of time off. But all of us have our faults, even doctors.

I know I have fewer injuries at 30 miles a week. I know that at 40 to 45 miles per week, I am still relatively injury-free. At 55 to 65 miles per week, I need much more stretching and much more time to recover from my runs. At 70 to 80 miles a week, I am often grouchy and sore. Between 80 and 90 miles, I am *always* grouchy, *always* sore.

But I run as far as I do because I am a dreamer. Dreams are the stuff of hopes and ideas, the stuff of heroes. Show me a person without dreams, and I will show you a failure. I dream of times gone by, of things I should have said and done, of races past and races to be run, of battles I have never fought. I think and dream as I run, and life becomes more real. The possibility of injury is part of that reality. I try not to take foolhardy risks, yet I accept the fact that daydreaming can be risky.

THE SADDEST ADVICE

Alfred Zuniga, 44, had four separate knee surgeries. He had been a long-distance runner, but noted that whenever he ran there was pain and swelling in the knee.

I felt a great amount of crepitation with motion of his knee joint, and X-rays showed degenerative arthritis in the knee. I told Al I was not sure I could do anything to help him, since the arthritis was advanced.

We tried orthotics and a heel lift. I ran with Al several times, and he looked like a good runner. He had a nice stride, but after 2 or 3 miles he felt so much pain in the knee that he had to stop.

Further examination showed limited range of motion in the knee. He tended to hyperextend the knee, flexing it beyond the straight position. Orthotics did not work in this case. They made his feet more comfortable but did little for the knee.

Zuniga visited an orthopedist who agreed with me that Al had degenerative arthritis in the knee joint and that he should find alternative sports. He was told to swim, ride a bike, or do whatever he could that did not hurt. He was also warned that if he continued running there was a chance it would speed the process of degeneration and increase the possibility of another surgical procedure.

I am often asked if running causes arthritis and what the longterm effects of running are. My usual answer is that running increases the range of motion and actually provides for more healthy cartilage in the joints rather than causing degeneration. Studies done in Finland have helped support this theory. I also feel that loss of motion which takes place in many people who have become sedentary is one of the main causes of stiffness. If the joint surfaces themselves are good, exercise will help preserve them. If there is a little bit of disuse arthritis, exercise will benefit the joint.

However, when there is gross post-traumatic arthritis of Zuniga's type, increased loading on the joint such as occurs during running will cause more degeneration. It is not often that I tell somebody to stop running and find another sport, but I had Al's future health in mind when I gave him this advice.

RUNNING STYLE

When you run, you should have more of a shuffling-type gait than a bounding, race-horse gait. It is important not to bounce up and down, since this causes the center of gravity to rise and fall too much, and creates inefficiency and excessive stress. It is important not to lean forward, or the front of your thigh will hit you at your pelvis and you will have an inefficient stride.

It is just as important not to lean too far backward. Run in an upright position. Think of your pelvis as holding water. If you lean forward, the water pours over the front of your body. If you lean backward, the water pours out the back of your body. Protect the water, not allowing it to spill out the front or back or to rise up and down too much and splash out.

What about foot contact? Most runners land on the outside of the heel. They do this because of the functional varus or bowlegged position which is natural when running. (In fact, most of the stress goes through your heel about one-fourth of an inch in front of the end of your heel. Some shoes are manufactured with so much slant there that they have no rubber under this area of maximum contact. These shoes should be avoided.)

Occasionally, a runner will have a high-arched foot with a dropped forefoot, meaning the forefoot is lower than the heel. This runner is often more comfortable landing on the ball of the foot. He may also benefit from a shoe with a very high heel or may need a Sporthotic device with an eighth-inch heel lift.

Some runners are more comfortable landing flatfooted or on the outside of the foot instead of the heel. This is okay. The important thing is to have a short stride and to have the foot under the center of gravity at zero acceleration. The biggest problem I see in style is overstriding.

UPS AND DOWNS

When running up hills, you may be more comfortable running on the ball of your foot. If you wish to get additional stretching of the muscles in the back of your leg, try running heel-foot-toe going uphill. You will notice this helps stretch out the backs of your legs. If, however, you are not limber in these structures, you may end up pulling a muscle, so be careful.

When going downhill, there is always a tendency to overstride. When this happens, the foot hits in front of the body and the ground pushes the foot and leg back, causing additional stress. Likewise, the knee is much more unstable while running downhill than uphill and this may increase the risk of injury.

When running turns or curves, it is easy to sprain an ankle by excessive twisting. When running on unfamiliar surfaces or on grass with potholes, you can twist, sprain, or even fracture an ankle. When running on trails with rocks, it is possible to hit a rock improperly and fracture a metatarsal or bruise a heel.

Running on the beach causes particular problems, because the sand may be so soft that your feet are not stable and there is excessive motion. The soft sand also may allow your heel to sink too far; this excessive lowering of the heel can strain the achilles tendon.

CHOOSING SHOES

Matt was prepared to spend a reasonable amount of money to outfit himself when he began running. He looked over all the running shoes on display at a local sports shop and picked out a colorful, very light pair. The shoes fit like a glove, and Matt was sure they were for him.

In the store, the shoes felt terrific. They were extremely flexible and did not irritate his feet. He was pretty sure these were the shoes worn by the winner of a three-mile race he had seen interviewed on the evening news a few days before. He bought the shoes.

Matt anxiously arose the next morning and proceeded to walk and jog for thirty minutes. The first day was not bad—a little soreness over the kneecap, but at least he made thirty minutes. He tried again the next day, and the kneecap hurt even when walking. After the run, however, there was no pain when Matt went golfing. He played racquetball later that afternoon, and he still felt no pain.

There was only pain when he ran in his new shoes. Each morning, Matt arose early and jogged and walked. Each morning, his knee hurt.

He came to me for advice. He wanted a biomechanical examination to show if there was something wrong in the way he was built. He had read this often causes the knee to hurt.

Matt's structure was sound. Biomechanically, he was more

normal than most people I see. Then, I looked at his shoes. I told him they were racing flats designed for running on the ball of the foot. They were certainly not for beginners like himself. They offered no arch support, were unstable, and were meant only for running at high speed.

Matt's problem was not with his body but with his shoes. I told him to get a proper pair of training shoes, jotting down the names of three models which might fit his foot well and offer adequate support and stability.

Matt complied. His pain disappeared. Perhaps if he had seen the *last-place* runner on the television show instead of the winner he would have chosen proper shoes the first time around.

I maintain that there is no perfect running shoe for all people and that the worst shoe for one runner might be the best shoe for another runner.

When shoes are evaluated, it is assumed that the average runner will be using these shoes and that an average runner has about a size 9 foot, runs 35 to 40 miles a week, and tends to run no faster than 7½ to 8 minutes per mile. This runner weighs 155 pounds. Using this average runner as a model there are various criteria for excellence in shoes:

● The shoes should have rubber which absorbs contact stress but yet does not fatigue. The thickness of rubber under the heel for a training shoe should be from three-quarters to one inch. The difference between the heel lift and the padding under the ball of the foot should allow a half inch to three-fourths inch lift of the heel. A training shoe should have three-eights to one-half inch of rubber padding under the ball of the foot.

● It is important for the shoes to have flexibility at the metatarsophalangeal joint, so that excessive strain does not take place in the posterior musculature.

● The toe box should not put pressure on the toes themselves and cause subungual hematoma. Likewise, the toe box should be round so as not to cause deviation of the great toe, causing hallux valgus or rubbing on the fifth toe.

● The outsole should provide for good traction and good wear, yet absorb shock.

● The upper should conform to foot deformities and allow for breathing so that excessive sweating does not take place.

● The tie pattern should allow for even distribution of pressure over the dorsum of the foot and yet not cause excessive strain on the dorsal tissue, or cause nerve entrapment or impingement.

● The heel cup should be firm and grasp the heel well to help prevent abnormal pronation and supination, yet should allow for a normal motion to take place.

● There should be some padding above the achilles tendon.

● Shoes with a flare on the heel above three inches are useful for lateral instability of the foot and ankle, but may cause knee problems in some people.

● The appropriate price range for a training shoe should be between $20 and $35. More expensive shoes in the $35 to $45 price range may be used, but may not offer any distinct advantage over the cheaper shoes.

SHOE FITTING

Shoes should be fitted so that there is one-fourth inch between the longest toe and the end of the shoe. The shoes should always be fitted for the bigger foot, not the smaller. The smaller foot slides forward in the shoe and one-eighth-inch felt can be applied under the tongue of the shoe to prevent this. If you have pain on the top of the foot because you tie your shoes too tight so you won't slide in the shoe, use sponge rubber under the tongue. If laces are irritating the top of your foot, skip a notch then cross over.

SHOE WEAR AND REPAIR

We used to think that abnormal shoe wear should be immediately repaired with a glue gun or some other preparation. I'm beginning to think this should be done very cautiously. If you put too much shoe glue or goo on the outside of your heel where you are wearing it down, you may reverse what your body is trying to achieve. In other words, by wearing down the outside of the heel, you have formed your own "varus wedge." Many runners notice that they have fewer overuse injuries once they have done this than when they have new shoes.

The best thing to do is to use a *small amount* of replacement material and to apply it regularly so you don't have a big gob on the back of your shoe. Once you get too much, this becomes a dominant portion of your heel and absorbs shock poorly. It also may cause you to pronate too much due to uneven application of the glue, and this can cause overuse injuries.

Remember that rubber fatigues. When the rubber on the bottom of your shoe starts losing its resiliency, then your shoes are not absorbing shock the way they should. It is time to get new shoes.

Too many runners send their shoes to be resoled, and only the outsole is replaced. The midsole, which absorbs shock, has fatigued rubber and the shoes are worthless. If you are going to have your shoe heels taken care of, be sure to have the entire heel replaced.

DO ORTHOTICS WORK?

Research done at my office in Hayward, California, and at California State University in Hayward has shown that podiatric biomechanical control increases the efficiency of the lower extremity and decreases overuse injuries. Information was gathered from nearly four thousand runners who have entered my sports medicine practice. Eighty-five to 90 percent of the overuse-related injuries of the lower extremity have responded to orthotic foot control. (We generally use a Sporthotic device which has flexible material and does not irritate the foot, but which guides the foot to assume a functionally neutral position during running activities.)

High-speed motion-picture photography was used to analyze runners with and without various forms of foot control. It was found that the foot was a more efficient lever system with orthotic control. Likewise, the running stride and angle of gait became more efficient. Further studies utilizing electrodes in various muscle groups measured the firing potential of these groups. As the sophistication of orthotic foot control increased, so did the efficiency of the lower extremity as demonstrated by electromyographic patterns. Testing with accelerometers showed that the foot absorbed shock better when it functioned around a neutral position, and shoes with good shock-absorbing properties complimented the orthotic foot control to protect the athlete from hard, unyielding surfaces.

The reason runners may need orthotics is that they have a functional varus, meaning they are more bowlegged in running than in walking. During walking, the feet are far apart. In running, one foot lands where the other foot was and gives a zero base of gait. This functional varus is particularly important on manmade surfaces. Our lower extremities were not designed for modern surfaces, yet the only place we can safely run at many times of the year and in many cities is on the roads or hard trails. Thus, we land on the outside of the foot, and as the foot flattens to reach the ground the leg internally rotates. This causes the foot and leg to be an unstable structure.

An orthotic merely fills the gap between the unyielding surface and the foot. It helps balance the foot so that the muscles and tendons can position the joints to use their own intrinsic strength. Orthotics, then, strengthen the lower extremity and teach you to run properly.

Do you need orthotics? The surface you use, your mileage, and your degree of biomechanical deformity are all factors in that decision. Let your sports podiatrist help you decide.

CORTISONE

I feel that cortisone definitely has a place in sports medicine. There are basically two types of injectable cortisone. One is short acting and is a soluable phosphate solution; the other is long acting, and is a repository acetate. I prefer to use a mixture of both to cut down the possibility of having the body flare up from the cortisone injection. The acetate is actually a crystal and somebody can get a flare from having crystals injected into the body.

When would I use cortisone? I like to use cortisone one week following ankle sprains in the sinus tarsi, or under the outer ankle bone if there tends to have been a serious sprain. I likewise use cortisone for injecting neuromas or nerve problems between the toes.

I try not to give more than two separate cortisone injections and have them spaced weekly. I have used cortisone injections for chronic achilles problems, meaning that the problems are at least two weeks old. I usually use no more than one injection for achilles problems, inasmuch as cortisone may weaken the tendon. Following a cortisone injection in the achilles tendon sheath, the runner is told not to stretch or strain the tendon for at least three weeks, to stay off hills and run moderately on flat surfaces.

Cortisone injections are of use whenever there is chronic inflammation or scar tissue. Cortisone may dissolve the scar tissue. The bad effect of cortisone, however, is that it also dissolves fat; repeated injections of cortisone may decrease the protective fat layer underneath the skin. Cortisone likewise weakens tissue as it softens tissue, and it may weaken healthy as well as diseased tissue.

Cortisone is most effective for bursitis. It is a marvelous drug for treating stone bruise, heel bursitis, or heel neuroma problems. It is also an excellent drug for joint pain if used with discretion. It is the treatment of choice for rheumatoid arthritis or gout in a major joint.

Cortisone is most damaging when given to someone who should be resting but continues working out hard, and actually damages his own tissue. Cortisone injections given in the manner described above have relatively little effect on the body as a whole. Massive doses of cortisone may be given once or twice with no effect on the adrenal gland. Cortisone pills given over a long period of time, however, will depress the adrenal glands and for this reason I tend not to use cortisone orally.

In conclusion, I feel that cortisone is a useful drug in sports medicine—if used by people who have a proper knowledge of function and know exactly what they wish to have the cortisone do. Likewise, cortisone can be abused just as orthotics can be abused or training methods can be abused.

SKIN AND NAIL PROBLEMS

Athletes often neglect their foot hygiene. You should have an ample supply of foot powder at home to sprinkle into running shoes and socks. After bathing or taking a shower, I usually walk around the house in a pair of mocassins with some foot powder in them. I usually use one of the over-the-counter powders to guard against getting athlete's foot or fungal problems. If I am worried about blistering in a long race, then I will use Vaseline on my feet as a lubricant.

In the summer, many youngsters walk around barefooted and get little nicks in their feet. After getting these nicks, it is common for a virus to cause a plantar wart. These plantar warts should be attended to because they can spread to other parts of the body and cause painful problems. It is best to be nonaggresive in treating a wart. I like to use a topical antiwart medication. My athletes apply this every night, or every other night if it causes irritation. Sooner or later, the warts go away. Vitamin A also helps warts go away, and my athletes are told to eat two carrots a day.

Toenail problems often are caused by shoes. Shoes with a shallow toe box cause pressure on the toenails, and the toenails may turn black and blue. This is actually a subungual hematoma, meaning that there has been bleeding under the toenail. The toenails may then become deformed, thickened or fall off. If there is pressure on the toenails, slit the toebox of your shoe so that the pressure is relieved, or else get shoes that fit properly. Shoes that are not wide enough in the toebox cause pain over the great toenails and can also cause ingrowing of the toenails. A podiatrist can initially take care of the ingrowing toenail problem, but then you should get proper shoes.

READING THE PAIN

When I am hurt, I usually know it. I can feel it coming on—tightness, aches and finally pain. I am an experienced runner and have learned to read my body. I know that fatigue leads to injury, that aches lead to pain, and that pain can progress to disaster. I know that running need not hurt and that you can prepare yourself to accept more stress without pain and injury.

But beginners do not always know this. I didn't, and neither did Alice. At the age of 24, she decided to become a runner. She assumed that running was beneficial and that the anticipated discomfort and pain would be richly rewarded by a fit body, increased vitality, and gradual loss of weight. Pain—a small price to pay!

So she ran, hard and far. Within one month, she was doing four miles a day; within two months, six miles a day. After two months of running, the ever-present, increasingly evident pain on the outside of her ankle became intense. She assumed that she had tendinitis, took aspirin, used an Ace wrap and ran. The pain increased.

After running for four more weeks, she jarred her foot when stepping in a hole during a run. The outer ankle pain became excruciating. Alice tightened the Ace wrap around her ankle, took more aspirin and ran some more.

She was forced to place most of her weight on the opposite foot. Two days later, the opposite foot was hurting so bad that she could not run. Walking was painful, and the foot was swollen on the top. She came to me for help.

X-rays confirmed my clinical diagnosis: stress fracture of the left third metatarsal, complete fracture of right outer ankle bone (fibula). There was evidence of a healing stress fracture and a new complete fracture through the healed fracture on the fibula, but there was no displacement of the fracture. Alice was lucky.

I immobolized and rested the ankle in a walking cast. The opposite foot was treated with a wooden stress shoe and taping to prevent movement. Alice would not run again for eight weeks. She could walk now without pain.

Chronic repetitive stress associated with pain had caused the ankle bone first to fatigue and then to break.

YOUTH

A 13-year old miler was brought to my office by his father. He had run a 4:51 mile and had pain in his right heel. His father said that he was still growing and had a great deal of potential.

My examination showed that there was a bone bruise on the bottom of the heel bone, the calcaneus. This is not unusual in young runners, because the bottom growth plate of the heel bone has not yet united with the main body of the heel bone. It is very common to have stress fractures of this growth plate called the calcaneal apophysis. X-rays were taken and there were lines and cracks suggestive of stress fractures of this portion of the heel.

Further examination showed that the muscles in front of the thigh that control the knee and are necessary for speed and power, the quadriceps, were somewhat weak. The pelvis was level. The patient had a rather high-arched foot with most of the stress being borne on the heel and under the metatarsal heads. There was a modest imbalance of both feet.

My diagnosis was a bone bruise or mild stress fracture of the heel along with relative weakness of the muscles in front of the thigh.

Treatment consisted of soft foot supports to pad the heel as well as strengthening exercises to build up the quadriceps. I told the young man that he should do his speed work on grass and not run on the track except for races.

The young man returned a week later and was extremely pleased with the soft supports and his training on the grass. He had run a 4:45 mile that week and, during it, had bruised the sesamoid bone under the ball of the right foot.

The sesamoid bone is a small bone under the first metatarsal head or under that portion of the foot where the great toe meets the ball of the foot. There are two such sesamoid bones which are easily traumatized, especially during jumping sports or running on hard surfaces. Fortunately, there was no fracture and this was easily treated with moleskin and taping. Even though there was a chance that he would outgrow permanent orthotics as his feet grew, his father requested a pair for his son.

The young miler was cast for permanent supports which were made over a mold of his foot. I prescribed flexible orthotics that would balance the heel and run the full length of the foot with a Morton's extension or pad under the great toe. I prescribed this flexible support for the young miler's training and racing activities, while I made a more rigid plastic support for everyday use.

With rigid orthotics, it's necessary to know the warning signs of too much or too little rearfoot control. Ideally, a rearfoot post allows the runner to contact on the outside of the heel anywhere from 2 to 4 degrees supinated and then to roll in to 2 to 4 degrees of pronation. Total motion is normally 6 to 8 degrees. The orthotics must allow this much motion, neither more nor less. Overuse injuries occur from errors in either direction.

The runner asked me if I thought that the soft supports, worn during the race, had helped his performance. I stated that the foot was a more stable lever with this type of foot support, especially with a Morton's extension under the great toe and it is conceivable that orthotics did help. What I am more concerned with, however, is whether orthotics make running more injury-free. It appears as though they do.

If my young patient's heel would not have improved with running on the grass and with soft supports, I would have explained to him that this is just not his season and that we could try taping his heel, but he shouldn't do anything with pain. I would have explained to him that teenagers often get stress fractures of growth plates, and the best treatment is to avoid hard surfaces and racing for a while. It is not unusual to force teenagers to sit out a season while their growth plates are uniting with the main bodies of the bones in their feet. They can usually do long, slow distance running, run on grass, ride a bike or swim, but racing will definitely cause further damage.

Our teenage miler's injury was rather moderate and responded well to our conservative treatment. In other cases, sprinting and hurdling has been postponed for a total season to allow for proper maturity and growth.

AGE

Thelma is 72 years old and walks thirty or forty minutes daily. She visits my office monthly for routine care of her calluses and corns, and adjustments to her orthotics.

She has had foot pain, knee pain, and hip pain. She had been an avid walker before this pain, but before seeing me, her pain had prevented her from walking her usual thirty to forty minutes per day. She went to her family physician who told her she probably had arthritis and would probably have to stop walking. He sent her to a specialist.

The specialist examined Thelma and told her to stop walking. He told her there was no use walking with pain, that she had arthritis, that she would get only worse if she used her joints too much.

Thelma returned to her family doctor complaining that her feet hurt and wondered if there was someone who could help her. He referred her to a podiatrist.

I examined Thelma from her hips to her toes and saw that her feet were moderately flattened and that her legs rolled in as her feet flattened, and her kneecaps also rolled in. But when she walked, her kneecaps rolled in and out. This rolling of the kneecaps to the outside of her legs was causing Thelma's knee pain.

I examined her knees and found that she had no arthritis at all—her knees were stable; there was no sign or symptom of grating in her joints. I confirmed this by taking X-rays of her knees that I and a colleague reviewed and found nothing wrong with the knees.

Her hips also appeared to be entirely within normal limits with the exception of some added strains secondary to the internal rotation of the legs concurrent with the overpronation of the feet. Thelma was a little overweight, so it was normal for her feet to flatten when a bit more weight was added to them.

Thelma also had complaints common with older people who have been wearing tight shoes all their lives. Thelma had mild bunions and some ingrowing of her toenails. She also had calluses under her second and third metatarsal heads and very painful calluses over her fifth toes. It was obvious when Thelma was standing that most of her weight was being borne by the second and third metatarsals. She had a Morton's foot with a short first metatarsal and great toe which bore weight poorly and transferred her weight to the adjacent two and three metatarsal heads. The fifth toes were likewise being forced into the shoes, causing them to be bent or contracted. These "hammertoes" had painfully thickened areas of skin called calluses. Under the calluses were small sacs, called bursa, which were like deep blisters full of inflammatory fluid.

I took X-rays of Thelma's feet that showed some bony deformity of the fifth toes, the bent great toe, and bunion, but no real arthritis. I told Thelma I thought we could have some good results by making her soft temporary supports to see if that helped her feet, knees and hips.

A week later, Thelma was elated. Her knees and hips had stopped hurting, and her feet felt good. The only things still hurting were her fifth toes. I told Thelma that her fifth toes were bent and would not straighten because of long years of pressure in tight shoes. I suggested that we straighten her toes in the office, utilizing the minor surgical suite that we had, under local anesthesia. We would do one foot at a time and she would not miss any time from her walking activities.

She agreed to this. Surgery on the right foot went extremely well, so we did the left foot three weeks later. Thelma was now walking her usual thirty to forty minutes a day, after more permanent orthotics were made for her. I sent a report to her doctor that her feet were doing well, as were her legs, knees and hips. He was surprised, but pleased.

Thelma just called. The running shoes I recommended she wear are fantastic for walking, at last a shoe for senior citizens. Her knees do not hurt, her hips do not hurt, and her feet do not hurt.

She told me "You know doctor, when your feet feel good, you feel good all over."

I told her I knew. I just wish other people did.

Acknowledgments

I would like to thank those who helped me with this book:

* Peggy Ritter, for the massive job of typing she has done.

* The editor on the project, Joe Henderson, who has been my friend and cohort.

* The illustrator, Dr. Stan Newell from Seattle.

* My family—my wife Jan and my children Mark, Ali, and Kari—for their indulgence in allowing me time away from them to do this work.

* Dedicated to my parents—Ruth and Leonard Subotnick. Only now do I appreciate the trials and tribulations of parenthood. Thanks Mom and Dad.

About the Author

Steve Subotnick was among the first to recognize that most running injuries begin in the feet, and to conclude that the foot specialist is the runner's first line of defense against disability.

Dr. Subotnick, a runner himself since the early 1970s, competes frequently in marathons and shorter races. He knows both from personal and professional experience how runners get hurt and get well. Hundreds of athletes have visited him at his Hayward, California office, and dozens of new doctors have learned sports medicine from him in his classes at the California College of Podiatric Medicine in San Francisco.

This is Dr. Subotnick's third book, following *Podiatric Sports Medicine* and *The Running Foot Doctor*. He serves as podiatric consultant for *Runner's World* magazine and has contributed to a number of professional journals.

Dr. Subotnick, his wife Jan and their three children—Mark, Kari and Ali—live in Hayward, California.

About the Illustrator

Dr. Stanley G. Newell is a sports podiatrist in Seattle, Washington, where he lives with his wife and children. He is a graduate of the California College of Podiatric Medicine and a Fellow of the Academy of Poiatric Sports Medicine. He has illustrated all of Steve Subotnick's previous books.

Index

Recommended Reading

Runner's World Aerobic Weight Training Book by Edwin Sobey and Gary Burns. A complete view of weight training through elaborate aerbic exercise programs. To complement bicycling, gymnastics, canoeing — the whole gamut. Paperback, $9.95

Runner's World Massage Book by Ray Hosler. A down-to-earth guide to body massage that treats the physiological as well as the psychological and philosophical. Paperback, $9.95

Runner's World Indoor Exercise Book by Richard Benyo and Rhonda Provost. The book that shows the beginner how to develop a sensible system in the comfort of his or her own home. Paperback, $9.95

Runner's World Advanced Indoor Exercise Book by Richard Benyo and Rhonda Provost. For committed exercisers — an extensive program for body strengthening and flexibility. Paperback, $9.95

Runner's World Stretching Book by Nell Weaver. A new approach to conditioning incorporating flexibility, speed, balance, agility, coordination, endurance and grace. Paperback, $9.95

Runner's World Vitamin Book by Virginia DeMoss. From Vitamin A to Zinc — consumers are offered an inside report on this ever-increasing market. Spiral-bound, $11.95

Complete Marathoner by the editors of *Runner's World*. The book that marathoners use for advice on training, equipment, first aid, pacing, special diets and dealing with extreme temperatures. Paperback, $8.95

Complete Runner II, edited by Bob Anderson. Information on injury prevention, acccessories, diet, training and competition — designed for sprinters, milers, marathoners and joggers. Hardback, $14.95

New Exercises for Runners by the editors of *Runner's World*. A revolutionary exercise program for athletes and fitness enthusiasts at different levels. Paperback, $4.95

Serious Runner's Handbook by Tom Osler. Written in a question-and-answer format, ultramarathoner Osler deals with training methods, shoes, diet techniques and tactics. Paperback, $5.95

Runner's World Yoga Book by Jean Couch. Achieving optimum physical and psychological flexibility with this completely illustrated book of yoga exercise programs. Spiral, $11.95

Jog, Run, Race by Joe Henderson. Leads the reader through several new beginnings — from walking to jogging, jogging to running, running to racing. Each beginning has a specific day by day progress guide. Paperback $5.95

The Complete Diet Guide: For Runners and Other Athletes, from the editors of *Runner's World*. How the athlete can use his diet to better advantage is the basis of this book. Areas addressed: Weight control, drinks, fasting, natural vs. processed food, vegetarian diets and more. Paperback $5.95

The Complete Woman Runner by the editors of *Runner's World*. Covering everything from getting started to entering competition once the body is properly conditioned, the book also contains a section on the mind and body of the woman runner: her potential and aptitudes. Hardback $12.00

Living Longer and Better by Harold Elrick, M.D., James Crakes, Ph.D., and Sam Clarke, M.S. The authors believe that traditional medical practice has mistakenly concentrated on the treatment rather than the prevention of disease. This book stresses preventing disease through proper diet, exercise. Paperback, $5.95

Dr. Sheehan's Medical Advice for Runners by Dr. George Sheehan. Here's Dr. Sheehan's first book designed to help you stay injury free. Dr. Sheehan feels that many running ailments are self-inflicted and therefore are preventable if we find and eliminate the cause. Hardback $11.95

Available in fine bookstores and sport shops, or from:

ANDERSON WORLD, INC.

Box 159, Mountain View, CA, 94042

Include $1.00 shipping and handling for each title (Maximum $3.00)